רודל רוד

Generation to Generation

Landsman Family History 1870 – 2018

WRITTEN AND RESEARCHED BY
ESTHER AND ROSLYN LANDSMAN

ISBN: 978-1-5356-1644-7

Mom, this book is your dream. Your persistence and perseverance over the last fifteen years to complete this project before even more details are lost forever has been an inspiration. Dad, I will never forget your patience with me while I pried as many details as possible from you about your childhood. Your fingerprints, quiet ways, and wise words are sprinkled throughout the book. It has been an honor and privilege to have spent so many wonderful hours and days with both of you to make your dream a reality.

Thank you for this amazing gift; I will cherish it always.

– Roslyn

Contents

Introduction

Family
History
Journeys
Luck

This is a book about our family—how history shaped it, how
journeys created it, and how luck played its own part. It is for
our children, our grandchildren, and all who come after. You
may read this as a young or grown child, or as a parent sharing the
story with your own children. As I researched material for this book,
I realized how much of our family's past is unknown, how many
details are lost, never to be recorded. I wanted to document as much
as possible for you and future generations.

It begins almost one hundred and fifty years ago in Eastern
Europe. Today's world seems small, with instant access to
information and fast modes of travel. I've lived in the same city
my whole life, yet my father and my maternal grandfather both
journeyed between two continents and three different countries in
the early 1900s, and Andre immigrated to Canada after World War
Two, when he was sixteen.

Even though I understood why they immigrated to Canada,
I thought you might have a lot of questions about why they
would want to leave Europe, where there were established cities,

infrastructure, and industry. At that time in Canada, especially the western parts, the country was not developed at all, and still mostly inhabited by the native Indians and Inuit.

There was little religious tolerance in Europe, which forced Jews to migrate extensively. From Spain to Portugal to Turkey and throughout Eastern Europe, Jews were attacked, banished, and forced to choose between death and converting to the prevailing religion. Homes and religious buildings were often destroyed. Sometimes the Jews moved voluntarily in search of more tolerant communities, but often they were forced to move, and their new situation may have been no better.

Russia in particular was a place where Jews had lived since the 1600s. In 1791 Catherine the Great of Russia created the Pale of Settlement, an area along Russia's western border, and forced most Jews to live within its confines.

Although Jews were permitted to live in this annex, there were many restrictions on what they were allowed to do. In the 1800s, there were more than five million Jews—almost half of the world's Jewish population—living in The Pale in small townships known as shtetls.

As The Pale was reduced in size by the prevailing government— though not in population—living conditions worsened and restrictions increased. Among these were limitations on travel, cancellations of land-settlement privileges, years of compulsory military service, quotas for admission of Jews to high schools and universities, and the prohibition on Jews voting in local elections. In 1881 the assassination of Czar Alexander II instigated a wave of government-condoned physical attacks on the Jews, known as pogroms[1], leaving thousands dead and homeless. These restrictions and the accompanying persecution provided the impetus for mass emigration.

Although my paternal and maternal families came to Canada via different routes, both were trying to escape the persecution in The Pale and create a better life for themselves and their children.

– Esther

---

1. "A pogrom is a violent riot aimed at massacre or persecution of an ethnic or religious group, particularly one aimed at Jews. The term originally entered the English language to describe 19th- and 20th-century attacks on Jews in the Russian Empire (mostly within the Pale of Settlement in present-day Ukraine); similar attacks against Jews at other times and places also became retrospectively known as pogroms." ("Category: Pogroms," Wikipedia.)

Harry Reinhorn.

Chapter One:
My Grandfather, Harry Reinhorn

Harry Reinhorn, my grandfather, grew up in Jassy, Romania, during the late nineteenth century. He was born in 1874. As I mentioned in the introduction, there were many restrictions being implemented by the government against the Jews, and most Jewish boys were not allowed to go to high school. Consequently, in 1890, when Harry was about sixteen, his family came up with the money for him to travel to Paris to continue his education. He did go to Paris, but instead of enrolling in school, he boarded a ship—the SS *Ohio*—bound for America and landed in Ellis Island in June of that year. I think he would have taken a train from Jassy to Paris, but who, if anyone, made arrangements for where he was going to live and go to school? What kind of communication did he have with his family? I can imagine him, in Paris, with no future, no prospects, and no way to earn a living, taking the risk to go to America. I always heard he was an adventurer and making those decisions at sixteen proves it.

SS *Ohio*, the ship Harry sailed on from Paris to New York in 1890.

He landed with few clothes and no money. He wandered the streets of New York and slept under wagons when he could. Some New Yorkers befriended him, and he got a job at a sweatshop operating a sewing machine. The shop must have been very warm and crowded. Exhausted and probably hungry after wandering the streets, he fell asleep at his machine the first day, and of course was immediately fired. Undaunted, and with the same spirit that got him to America, he walked up and down the streets of Manhattan, knocking on doors and asking in Yiddish for a job. By chance, a German-speaking steward at Delta Kappa Epsilon (DKE), a private gentleman's club, answered the knock on the door and asked Harry if he could speak German. Harry spoke Yiddish, a Jewish language based on German, and he answered brazenly that he was fluent in the language and was hired as the steward's assistant. DKE was founded at Yale College in Connecticut in 1844, and the New York Club in 1885. What a coincidence that Avery and Alex's father went to Yale University in the seventies. They often stay at the Yale Club in New York, where Harry worked. The club's motto was "Where the candidate most favored was he who combined in the most equal proportions the gentleman, the scholar, and the jolly good fellow." How fortunate that Harry wound up working and living in such an educated and stable environment. The wealthy fraternity members were delighted by his engaging personality and virtually adopted him, teaching him to read and write English. He spent eight years at the fraternity house and saved five thousand dollars, which he used to return to Romania in search of a Jewish bride. You have to remember that if he saved five thousand dollars in those days, he must have saved every single penny he earned. I'm guessing that tips made up a large part of his savings.

Harry's intention was to return to America with his bride, so he applied for US naturalization and a US passport in New York before he left. His passport application states that he expected to be in Romania for about twelve months.

Back in Jassy, he met and married Theophelia Groper, a plump and exceptionally pretty tailor's daughter, known to everyone as Toby and sometimes Tafalika. Throughout this book you will notice many inconsistencies with names. It seems as though each official spelled a name differently. Even my mother's name is wrong on her birth certificate. It says Eva rather than Evelyn.

6

Family Name	Given Name or Names
REINHORN	HARRY

R 565

Title and Location of Court

U. S. DISTRICT COURT, NEW YORK, N.Y.

Date of Naturalization	Volume or Bundle No.	Page No.	Copy of Record No.
MAR. 18, 1898	668	—	639

Address of Naturalized Person

105 W. 29 ST.   N.Y. CITY

Occupation	Birth Date or Age	Former Nationality
STEWARD	AUG. 16, 1874	ROUMANIAN

Port of Arrival in the United States	Date of Arrival
N.Y. N.Y.	JUNE 10, 1890

Names, Addresses and Occupations of Witnesses To Naturalization

1 SIGMUND SINDEL   175 ALLEN ST.
2   N.Y. CITY M'F'G

Above: Harry's certificate of naturalization.

Left: Harry's passport application. He is described as being five feet three and a half inches (instead of five feet, five and a half inches), with a high forehead and a rather broad nose.

7

Theophelia Groper Reinhorn, Harry's new bride. It is too bad that I don't have any pictures from their wedding, though it would have been difficult for them to transport to Canada.

I know the date they were married, February 28, 1898, because the date is engraved on her wedding band, which I wear on a chain around my neck when I travel as a good-luck charm to keep me safe. As is typical in Jewish tradition, the ring is a plain gold band. Tina, my daughter, Erica, my granddaughter, and I were all married with this ring.

Still in Jassy, and not long after the birth of their first daughter, Ernestina (always known as Tiana), Harry became involved in a movement that allowed Jews to farm and own their own land and homes in Canada. This was the Dominion Lands Act, an 1872

Canadian law that aimed to encourage the settlement of Canada's prairie provinces. In order to settle the area, Canada invited mass immigration by European and American pioneers, as well as settlers from eastern Canada. It echoed the American homestead system by offering ownership of one hundred and sixty acres of land free (except for a small registration fee of ten dollars) to any man over eighteen or any woman heading a household.

At the same time, Baron Maurice de Hirsch, a German-Jewish philanthropist, was devoting much of his time to schemes for relief of Jews in lands where they were persecuted and oppressed. In 1882, he gave the Russian government two million pounds to develop a system of secular education to be established in the Jewish settlements of The Pale. The Russian government took his money but never allowed any foreigner or Jew to be involved in administering the funds. Basically, they took the money but never did anything for the Jews with it. Hirsch then resolved to devote his money to an immigration and colonization plan, which would afford the persecuted Jews opportunities to establish themselves in agricultural colonies outside of Russia. He founded the Jewish Colonization Association as an English society (a charitable organization in today's words) with a capital of two million pounds, and in 1892 he added an additional seven million pounds. When his wife died in 1899 the capital was increased to eleven million pounds. This enormous fund was in its time probably the greatest charitable trust in the world. It was a combined effort of the Jewish Colonization Association, which was able to give each family two hundred dollars, and the Dominion Lands Act, which gave the Jews land and the opportunity to settle in Canada.

Harry became the colonization agent for a group of forty families, about one hundred people, who chose to settle in Saskatchewan, Canada. The Romanian travelers set out on their odyssey in 1902. Harry would have been twenty-seven when he, Toby, and Tiana, their infant daughter, headed out with just their clothes, their Sabbath candlesticks, and their separate sets of copper pots and pans for meat and dairy dishes so they would be able to keep kosher. They left in high spirits, singing songs, and made up jingles in Yiddish—*Go dear Jews into the wide world, in Canada you will make your fortune.* (Sounds a bit corny, but this is really what they might have been singing.) I don't know how they got from Romania to Liverpool, where the ship departed. From the ship's manifest, I know they were on the SS *Manitoba* with some other members of their family.

SS *Lake Manitoba*, the ship Harry sailed on with his family to Canada.

They were not singing so cheerfully when they eventually reached their destination in Qu'Appelle, literally the end of the Canadian Pacific Railroad. They were dismayed to find themselves on the barren and windswept Saskatchewan prairie, fifty miles northeast of what had originally been called "pile of buffalo bones." Somehow the travelers had to get from Qu'Appelle to Rostern, where they settled. I've heard stories of them going by foot, but since it's over two hundred and fifty miles, here is what I think happened. Their official landing location was Qu'Appelle as indicated on the ship's manifest. They

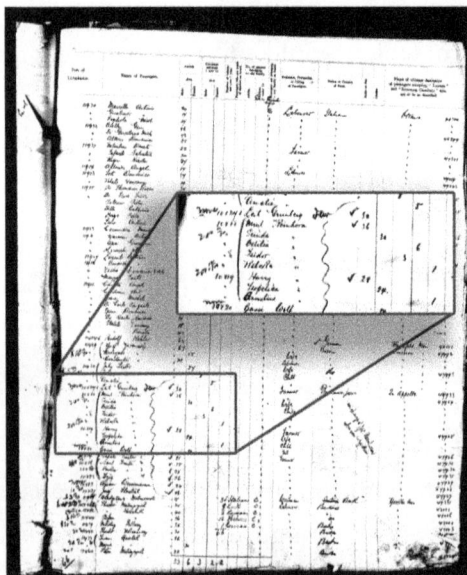

The ship's manifest provided proof that Harry and his family sailed on the SS *Lake Manitoba* in 1902, bound for Canada and a free life.

10

must have changed trains and gone from Qu'Appelle to Saskatoon and then by foot and horse and buggy the last forty miles to Rostern. This is where they applied for and received their land grant.

Harry's land grant certificate.

It's the summer of 1902 and here they are in Rostern. Toby was pregnant with Evelyn, my mother. Again, it's hard to know exactly what happened. Evelyn was born a few months later in October 1902. Evelyn always said she was born in their log house with the help of a midwife. A doctor had been called and had to travel fifteen miles by horse and sleigh, with two changes of horses along the way. He charged five dollars for his "house call" even though he arrived too late.

Rostern was so far north that even in early October there was enough snow to require a sleigh. You might be wondering why the land grant was dated January 1903 (after Evelyn was born). My guess is the land was allocated when they arrived in the summer of 1902. Building likely started right away in order to beat the harsh winter; however, the official paperwork did not come through until January.

The new immigrants had no farming experience. The local Cree Indians and the Métis took pity on them and showed them how to plow and build log huts. They plowed up a few acres for potatoes and put up some hay. Having arrived in the summer, they probably had just enough time to be ready for their first Canadian winter. How did they survive with no central heating? They slept on straw mats

Railway street in Rosthern, 1904.

on mud floors. Instead of down jackets they had fur suits. The stove in the kitchen would heat the hut and they rarely let the fire die out. By this time Harry was established as a peddler and traded with the Indians. I don't really know what he gave to the Indians, but in return for about twenty-five cents' worth of goods he received sacks of ermine furs. Once his family was outfitted with fur suits he probably sold the rest to the Hudson Bay Company. Their house had no electricity or plumbing. For toilet facilities, there was an outhouse. Needless to say, at forty degrees below zero you didn't always go to the outhouse. Using chamber pots was common. They survived a diphtheria epidemic and endured droughts, hail, and grasshopper plagues. (Sounds a bit like the ten plagues described in the

Another view of Rosthern in the early 1900's. You can see from these photographs that this was a small town, just being developed.

Passover Haggada). I know the diphtheria epidemic happened for sure. Harry and Theophelia had relatives in Chicago and New York whom they visited once or twice. They would have taken sleighs or a horse and carriage depending on the season and trains. On one trip, they were called back home for the children because of the epidemic.

Around 1905, Harry moved the family further north to an even more remote community, Duck Lake. Harry, by now fluent in French, English, and German as well as Romanian and Yiddish, had no trouble communicating with the four hundred Indians and Métis inhabitants of Duck Lake. Over the next few years he became a legendary figure: a Jewish peddler in fringed buckskin and moccasins. His winning ways were said to be irresistible, whether he was buying beaver pelts or selling dry goods and trinkets. He went through the four conventional stages of peddling in Duck Lake, first trudging on foot while hefting a heavy backpack hung with tin wares and other items strung around his neck. Next came a pushcart, followed by a horse and buggy. Finally, he rose to the pinnacle of the trade, which meant ownership of his own little general store, which he opened in Duck Lake. He was a master salesman, had a smile and a joke for everyone, and was a strong leader.

Theophelia's sister, Sabina and her husband, Herman Lazaresu, also settled in Duck Lake. They had been married in Romania and came to Canada in 1906 with their three children, Alfred, Edward, and Lucy, who was only six months old. I'm not sure when, but Lazaresu became Laxton. Roslyn, Tina, Susan, and Sam will remember Lucy and "beep bop Lou how do you do," favorites from Toronto.

Herman joined Harry as a peddler and then became

Sabina and Herman on their wedding day in Romania. The formality and detail of Sabina's dress and Herman's suit and top hat are wonderful to see.

13

assistant manager in his Duck Lake general store. The Reinhorns and Lazaresus were the only Jewish families in Duck Lake. They were very close and spent a lot of time together.

The Reinhorns and Lazaresus on an outing. I wish the picture was clearer, but my best guess is that Harry is in the middle driving, Toby is to the right and Evelyn is pictured in the bottom right corner of the carriage. Another item I think about when I look at this picture is how did they take care of their fancy clothes without all the conveniences like washing machines and dry cleaners that we take for granted today.

They were observant Jews in the sense that they never cleaned the house or lit a fire to cook on the Sabbath, but since there weren't enough Jewish men to form a minyan of ten, they were not able to have synagogue prayer services. This was the key reason why the two families moved to Saskatoon, where there was a Jewish community of about thirty families. Harry, the more enterprising of the two men, opened Reinhorn's Furniture Store on Second Avenue. Herman, the poet and scholar, worked as his manager. Harry's creative merchandising ideas helped propel the store's success.

The two sisters in Saskatoon. Sabina on the left and Theophelia (Toby) on the right. Their hats and fur stoles are fantastic.

Harry and Theophelia continued to expand their family. After Evelyn there was Abe, followed by twins. In 1909, when the twins, Ann and Arthur, were about three, they hired a housekeeper, Lucy Canon. She came by train from somewhere in the US. A few years later, in 1912, Theophelia's mother, Ella, immigrated to Saskatoon. At the time, she was seventy and a widow.

We all know that Harry was fluent in French. What is interesting is that Theophelia spoke French too, while everyone else in the family spoke only English. They could all read and write, including the housekeeper, Lucy.

While they lived in Saskatoon, Harry's home was always open for Friday night (Shabbat) dinners and all the Jewish holidays to anyone who didn't have a place to go. Sam Cowan, a young, handsome bachelor, was often present for these dinners. You'll hear more about Sam in another chapter but isn't it interesting how opening your home to strangers for Shabbat dinner played such an important role in our family.

Harry's store was across the street from the movie theatre and Harry used to lend the theatre pieces of furniture for movie sets and theatre productions in exchange for movie tickets. His daughter Evelyn, my mother, invited *all* her friends, instead of just one. The movie-theatre owner was not too happy having so many non-paying customers and spoke to Harry about it. That was the end of free tickets.

To wrap up, there was Tiana (born in Romania), Evelyn (conceived in Romania and born in Canada), Abe, then the twins, Ann and Arthur. Tiana not only finished high school, something neither of her parents were able to do, but went to the University of Saskatchewan and graduated with a liberal-arts degree. This was truly a significant accomplishment. Tiana was very popular with all the boys, but there just weren't many Jewish ones. Consequently, when Harry went to Toronto in 1921 to buy furniture for his store, he discreetly made inquiries about the availability of a prospective

The Reinhorn family in 1912. Top row from the left, Tiana, Evelyn, Theophelia, baby, Ann. Bottom row: Abe, Arthur and Harry. The baby died a few months after this picture was taken.

Jewish husband for his daughter. He was told about a bright and handsome fellow named Leon Koffler, also an immigrant from Romania. He seemed a good catch, as he was a professional, planning to open a drugstore on College Street, one of the main commercial arteries of Toronto's Jewish neighborhoods. It was carefully arranged that the couple should meet casually at a social gathering, where they did indeed "click." In 1922 Harry and Theophelia moved to Toronto with their entire family of three daughters and two sons. The Lazaresus soon followed in time to attend Tiana and Leon's wedding. Aside from them meeting casually at a social event in 1922, I don't know anything about how or if they got to know each other. Leon was living in Toronto and Tiana in Saskatoon. Did Harry get Leon to visit Saskatoon, or did Tiana accompany Harry to Toronto for his buying trips? We'll never know, but that was the beginning of our Toronto family.

My mother's brother Abe went on to graduate from the University of Toronto in 1929 and had a very distinguished career as a research and clinical ophthalmologist in the United States. When he was young, and the family still lived in Saskatchewan, he often traveled with his father to visit the Indians he was trading with, and many times they also administered medical aid. I think this is where his interest in becoming a doctor came from. Before he settled in the United States, he returned to Saskatchewan for a few years, where he worked at a tuberculin hospital for children. The facility treated Indian children free of charge, an early form of socialized medicine.

Harry passed away from a stroke in 1933 at the age of fifty-nine. This was right before a scheduled interview with a Canadian historian who was documenting the settlement of western Canada, so he was unable to give his account of settling in the west.

Sam and Evelyn, on their honeymoon in Atlantic City, June 1924.

Chapter Two:
My Parents, Sam and Evelyn

My father, Sam Cowan, one of eleven children, was born in 1889 in Russia to Ivor and Bessie Abromovici. His father was a "shochet," a religious Jew licensed and trained to slaughter mammals (mostly cows and sheep) and birds (mostly chickens) for food according to Jewish kosher dietary laws. Today we would call him a kosher butcher. In those days, being a shochet and Talmudic scholar would have given the family some prestige within the community. As I mentioned before, the Jews were subject to a variety of pogroms and all boys over thirteen had to serve in the Russian army. As a young family, Sam's parents secretly fled across the border into Romania to avoid this fate for their male children. Though there were few safe places for Jews to live, Romania was a better place than many other Eastern European countries during this time period. The journey was difficult and dangerous. Sam was probably five when they left. One story that was passed down in the family was that while crossing the Prut River, the border between Romania and the Russian empire, Sam's younger sister, Sophie (Uncle Len and Aunt Nettie's mother), started to cry. The others in the boat said they would throw her overboard if she didn't stop. Thank God she did, and they all arrived safely on the shore in Romania, settling in Negresti. I don't know much about Sam's years in Negresti; I never asked, and he never talked about it.

Even though life in Romania was better than in Russia, there was still no option for high school. So, like his future father-in-law, Harry, Sam came to Canada in March of 1904, just after he turned seventeen. His ship, the SS *Manitoba* (the same one Harry took in 1890), landed in New Brunswick, from where Sam made his way to Quebec City. I know you've heard stories of how people got their names when they came to America. Here's how it went for my father, who was registered on the ship's manifest as Schapsobe Abromovici. When the immigration officer asked Sam for his name, he replied, "Abromovici." The immigration officer, being French, could not pronounce that and kept repeating the question. When Sam realized that Abromovici wasn't going to work, he replied, "Kohen," his Israeli tribe name. That's how he got the name Sam Cowan. (At least the Anglicized version of his first name is correct.)

Like most Jews in Romania and throughout Europe, Sam's family lived in a small village. Everyone knew each other, and if you weren't related, you might be a Lantsman—the Yiddish word for "coming from the same place." It was an effective word-of-mouth network, supplemented with written correspondence. Sam's family got the name of a distant cousin living in Quebec City, and that is where he stayed when he first arrived.

Sam was not with them for very long and was encouraged to go out on his own. He too started peddling, selling pencils and other small objects. Peddlers had a significant role in supplying isolated populations with fairly basic and diverse goods such as pots and pans, blankets, horses, and the news. This was a common start-up business for immigrants and Sam was very successful. It would be similar to today's immigrants opening a convenience store or restaurant. After a few years, when he had earned enough, he traded in his pushcart for a horse and wagon to expand his sales area and increase the variety of goods he offered. He began selling to French farmers in and around Quebec City. It was quite an accomplishment for a young man to have his own horse and wagon. The French farmers were impressed with his hard work and good looks and often invited him to stay overnight and spend time with their daughters. Sam did not take them up on their offers.

In 1910, six years after his arrival in Canada and only twenty-two years old, Sam moved to Saskatoon. I don't know exactly what motivated that move, but Sam may very well have been influenced by the same massive immigration campaign that brought Harry to Saskatchewan. Once the railroad was complete, the small, isolated settlements quickly grew to villages and towns. By this time there was the business opportunity to serve the farmers who had settled there. He partnered with a Mr. Mallin and opened a menswear shop, the Blue Store.

Local History Room - Saskatoon Public Library

LH-4832-B

The Blue Store on the left in the 1920's.

Though I have few details about Sam's time in Saskatoon, I do know that the Jewish community was tight-knit. Sam was president of the Saskatoon Zion Hertzl society and local director of the Esther Robinson orphanage of Winnipeg. Sam, my father, and Harry, my (maternal) grandfather, knew each other. They both had retail stores and were active in the community. Sam was a frequent visitor at my grandparents' home, often coming for Shabbat dinner. I like to think Sam may have had his eye on Evelyn then, but she would have only been thirteen or fourteen at the time.

23

Evelyn and her sisters enjoying a beautiful day during the same time Sam was living in Saskatoon. Left to right - Tiana, a neighbour, Lucy, Evelyn and other neighbours. Tiana and Lucy are Evelyn's sisters.

At twenty-eight, he was again on the move. He sold his interest in the store in Saskatoon in 1916 and moved to Montréal. The Zion Hertzel society held a farewell celebration in his honor and presented him with a silver cigar case to commemorate his hard work.

In Montréal, he was partners with several others in the menswear manufacturing business for six more years. Around 1922, at thirty-four, he again struck out on his own and started Majestic Neckwear, manufacturing ties and mufflers (called scarves today). The first manufacturing facility was on 2010 St Laurence Blvd in the Grothe building,

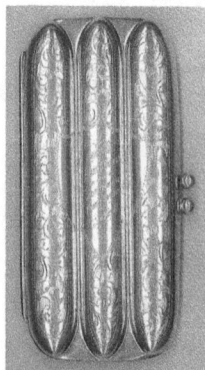

The cigar case he was presented with at his farewell dinner. I still have it today.

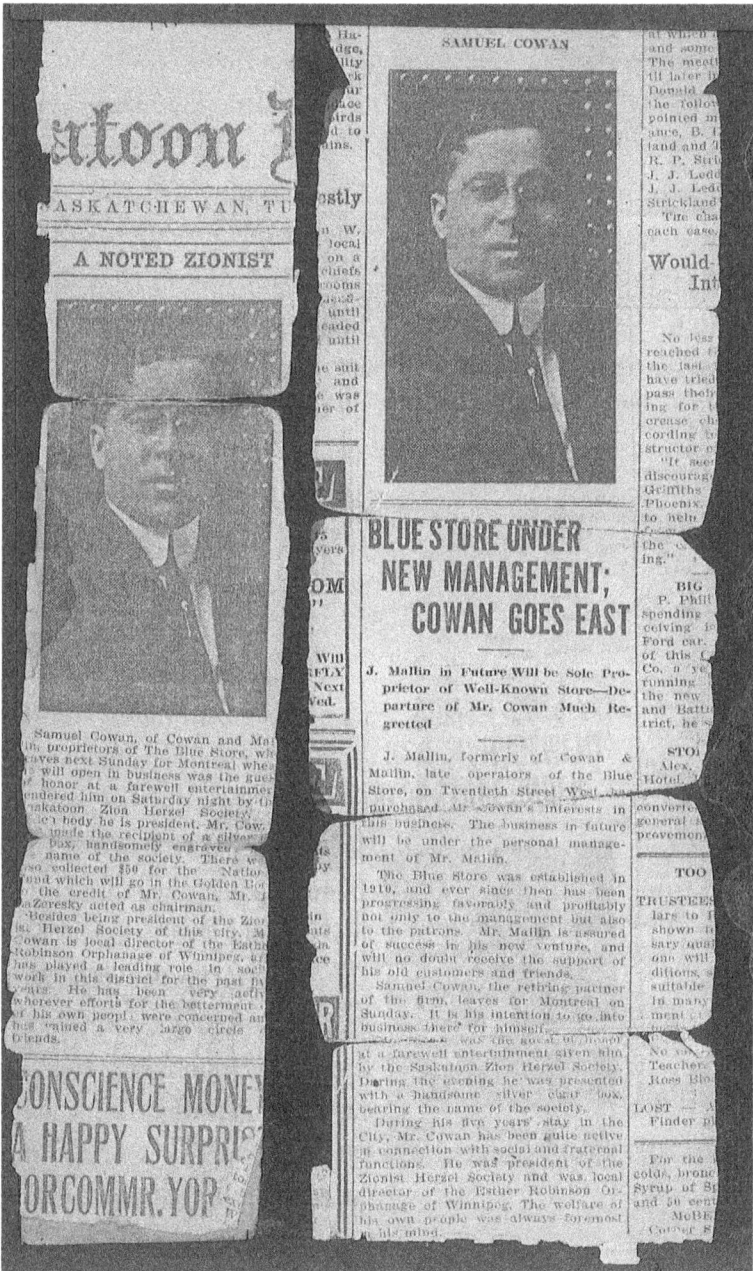

SAMUEL COWAN

A NOTED ZIONIST

BLUE STORE UNDER NEW MANAGEMENT; COWAN GOES EAST

J. Mallin in Future Will be Sole Proprietor of Well-Known Store—Departure of Mr. Cowan Much Regretted

J. Mallin, formerly of Cowan & Mallin, late operators of the Blue Store, on Twentieth Street West, purchased Mr. Cowan's interests in his business. The business in future will be under the personal management of Mr. Mallin.

The Blue Store was established in 1910, and ever since then has been progressing favorably and profitably not only to the management but also to the patrons. Mr. Mallin is assured of success in his new venture, and will no doubt receive the support of his old customers and friends.

Samuel Cowan, the retiring partner of the firm, leaves for Montreal on Sunday. It is his intention to go into business there for himself.

[...] at a farewell entertainment given him by the Saskatoon Zion Herzel Society. During the evening he was presented with a handsome silver cigar box, bearing the name of the society.

During his five years' stay in the city, Mr. Cowan has been quite active in connection with social and fraternal functions. He was president of the Zionist Herzel Society and was local director of the Esther Robinson Orphanage of Winnipeg. The welfare of his own people was always foremost in his mind.

ASKATCHEWAN, TU

Samuel Cowan, of Cowan and Mallin, proprietors of The Blue Store, who leaves next Sunday for Montreal where he will open in business was the guest of honor at a farewell entertainment tendered him on Saturday night by the Saskatoon Zion Herzel Society, of which body he is president. Mr. Cowan was made the recipient of a silver box, handsomely engraved with the name of the society. There was also collected $50 for the National fund which will go in the Golden Book to the credit of Mr. Cowan. Mr. J. Zeresky acted as chairman.

Besides being president of the Zionist Herzel Society of this city, Mr. Cowan is local director of the Esther Robinson Orphanage of Winnipeg, and has played a leading role in social work in this district for the past few years. He has been very active wherever efforts for the betterment of his own people were concerned and has gained a very large circle of friends.

CONSCIENCE MONEY

A HAPPY SURPRISE

OR COMMR. YOP

Two local newspaper articles written about Sam when he was leaving Saskatoon in 1916. They give a good description of his place and activities in the community.

25

which is now a historical landmark. I'll never know why he moved back to Montréal. Was he looking for a bigger community, or, like Andre (twenty-seven years later), did he realize there were significant opportunities in the bigger cities of Montréal and Toronto? I also find it interesting that people made such big moves across Canada in the early 1900s when travel was much more difficult than today. Harry went from Romania to New York, back to Romania, then to Saskatchewan, only to head east to Toronto. Sam went from Romania to Quebec to Saskatoon and then back east to Montréal.

Evelyn with her sisters in their backyard in Toronto. From the top clockwise - Tiana, Evelyn, Theophelia, Ann and Sabina. Theophelia was Evelyn's mother and Sabina was her aunt.

That same year, 1922, my maternal grandparents, Harry and Theophelia, along with all their children, moved to Toronto. The oldest, Tiana, married Leon Koffler. Next in line is Evelyn.

Two years later, in 1924, Evelyn married Sam Cowan in Toronto. She was twenty-two and Sam was thirty-six. How did that happen? He had a reputation of being a very eligible bachelor who did his fair share of dating in Montréal. Did he come looking for her, did he travel to Toronto frequently and keep up with his friends who had also moved from Saskatoon, or was it an arranged match—I'll never know. Remember that Sam knew Harry's family from his time in Saskatoon. Regardless of the origins of their relationship, they had a wonderful marriage and were truly in love.

Sam and Evelyn's marriage certificate. In addition to name, age and occupation the form asks for "condition in life" with only two options. For the groom it's bachelor or widower and for the bride it's widow or spinster!

Sam and Evelyn discussed the idea of moving Sam's new business to Toronto or keeping it in Montréal. My mother, Evelyn, assured Sam that Montréal would be wonderful and there was no reason for him to move his business. I continue to be amazed at everyone's independence, at their ability to pick up and start over in a new place without the security of old friends and family. After the wedding, the couple was off to Europe for their six-week honeymoon. They took the train to Atlantic City, where they spent some time in the New York area with Evelyn's cousins, who had emigrated from Romania and settled in New Jersey. They were in the millinery (hat) business. After time with family they boarded their ship in New York for a grand European tour.

The wedding announcement in the local newspaper.

Evelyn on their wedding day.

Sam on their wedding day.

Sam and Evelyn in Atlantic city at
the beginning of their honeymoon.

Evelyn and her brother Abe who was
living in the area and visited them in
Atlantic City.

When they returned they moved into an apartment on the corner
of Lajoie and Outremont, a vibrant and upscale Jewish community.
They had an active social life. With the significant migration of Jews
from Europe and Russia, family became important as new arrivals
tried to create a community for themselves. People counted as family
regardless of how distant or obscure the relationship was. Someone
could be family by virtue of being your mother's sister's brother-in-
law's nephew's son, or, just as often, you were considered family by
being from the same town or village.

Remember the cousins that Sam stayed with when he first
arrived? Well, they also had cousins who lived in Montréal, the
Kleinberg family. The Cowan's and the Kleinberg's developed a very
close relationship. Jenny and Lewis Kleinberg had eight children.
Evelyn became best friends with Queenie, one of the eight siblings.
The two families celebrated all the Jewish holidays together, from
Friday evenings to Passover Seders.

My parents travelled often, for both business and pleasure. Every two or three years they would go to Europe by ship. I know of two trips in particular, in 1931 and 1933. The first was on the *Duchess of Atholl*, which for a brief time held the record transatlantic crossing of six days and thirteen hours.

The second trip was on board sister ships—the SS *Bremen* eastbound, returning on the SS *Europa*. At the time of their construction, these were the two most advanced high-speed steam-turbine

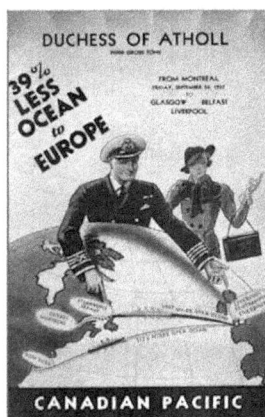

An advertisement for the Duchess of Atholl.

ocean liners of their day. Their record crossing time was four days seventeen hours.

Sam and Evelyn lounging on the deck.

Sam and Evelyn taking a stroll on the deck of the ship.

These were also the first ships to carry a small float plane, which was launched by a catapult to deliver mail. The plane would be launched about twenty miles away from port so that mail could be delivered before the ship's arrival. On her maiden voyage, she delivered eleven thousand pieces of mail.

Once they arrived they would start the trip with a visit to Manchester, looking for woolens for their muffler business. If it was winter, which was the case for the 1933 trip, they would need to keep putting schillings in the heater in their hotel room to keep warm, similar to feeding a parking meter. Evelyn, who was always susceptible to chills and colds, inevitably got sick. The next stop would be London, where Sam visited his sisters. Some of the other places they visited included Como, Italy, and Dusseldorf, Germany, where Sam bought silk for ties. On this trip, Sam's parents and two brothers travelled to Prague to meet him. He had not seen any of his family for almost thirty years, since he'd left Romania in 1904.

And always, there was a stop in Paris. These trips would be at least four to six weeks long. They packed in steamer trunks with lots of formal clothing, furs, and, of course, hats. No rolling suitcases back then! They also travelled to Toronto two or three times a year to visit Evelyn's family.

It was not typical for people in their circle of friends to travel by ship to Europe—let alone first class—on a regular basis. Nor was it typical to have a car, which Sam always did. I think one of the reasons they were able to afford these things is because Sam had his own business, where some of these expenses were covered and necessary.

Sam and Evelyn on their 1933 overseas trip. Sam is sitting on the donkey with Evelyn on the right. Sam's German agent and the agent's wife are on the left.

Left: Sam, in the center top row with his brothers and parents who travelled to Prague to meet him.

33

Back in Montréal, Sam and Evelyn had a large social circle. In those days, you actually knew all your neighbours, knew your family's friends, and knew your friends' families, along with the many business relationships you developed. Often the business relationships became personal as well. Everyone knew everyone! Sam continued to be very involved in his business and active in the Jewish community, both philanthropically and with leadership roles.

Fast-forward to 1934, ten years after Sam and Evelyn got married, when Harry passed away in Toronto. Sam and Evelyn are living on Sherbrooke Street in the Barat Court apartments. They joined the Shaar Hashomayim synagogue, which was now within walking distance. Business was doing well. Sam was known in the business community as an ethical, generous, and honest man. His word and reputation were everything to him. Evelyn took care of things in the apartment, was an excellent cook, and spent lots of time with friends. Remember that things took a lot longer to do then. There was no such thing as a quick trip to the grocery store or tossing dirty clothes into the washing machine. Keeping house was a full-time job.

When Evelyn was twenty-five she had a miscarriage. There were some complications and the doctors told the couple that future pregnancies would be life-threatening. This was very disappointing to them. All their friends were starting large families. Four or five years later, one of Evelyn's friends adopted a baby. This must have been an inspiration for them, as they too began inquiring about adoption. And in April of 1935 they arrived home with six-month-old Esther in tow.

Esther Landsman.

Chapter Three:
Esther

Here I am, adopted into my new family in Montréal. I was born October 7, 1934. I know few details surrounding my birth and adoption and truly never felt the need or desire to learn more. I have a vague recollection of my mother mentioning that a Rabbi Klein in New York helped facilitate the adoption, and I never felt the need to know who my birth parents were.

The only birth certificate I have is from our synagogue, the Shaar Hashomayim, listing Sam and Evelyn Cowan as my parents. I do know I was born in the United States, somewhere in New York, and that my parents had to travel to New York to get me. Was everything arranged through the mail, or did my parents first visit the orphanage or facility where I was? Either way, it meant a long train trip, possibly overnight. On April 4, 1935, when I was just six months old, I crossed the border from New York to Montréal and am listed as traveling with my foster parents Mr. and Mrs. S. Cohen (still not getting the names right).

Me at about
six-months-old.

I'm sure they had a nurse with them when they came to pick me up, as I can't imagine them without one. In those days everyone had a full-time, live-in nurse for their babies. Even when I later had my own children there was a nurse, and moms didn't have to get up in the middle of the night for a feeding.

I was named after both my grandfathers, Iser on my father's side and Harry on my mother's. Since I was a girl (obviously), the names

My Canadian Immigration Services border crossing document.

became Esther and Harriet. It might have been hard to decide which name to use as the first one, but since Iser had passed away first and because Evelyn's brother Arthur had recently had a girl they'd named Harriet, the decision was made to name me Esther Harriet.

My parents often rented a country house for the summer, usually with a group of three or four other friends with their families. They would go on weekends and for the two weeks in July when the factory was closed for summer vacation. My first summer was spent in Alexandria, Ontario. It would have been only two months after I arrived in Montréal, the summer of 1935, when I was eight to ten months old. Maybe that's where my desire to travel comes from. My grandmother Toby spent summers with us, after her husband, Harry, my grandfather, passed away in Toronto two years earlier.

From our first summer in Alexandria with my mother Evelyn.

Don't you love the bathing suit
my father Sam was wearing in this
photograph with me?

Here I am with my grandmother
Theophelia and my father Sam.

At this time we were living in
the Barat Court apartments on
Sherbrooke Street. I'm in the park
close by were I often played. I was
one and a half.

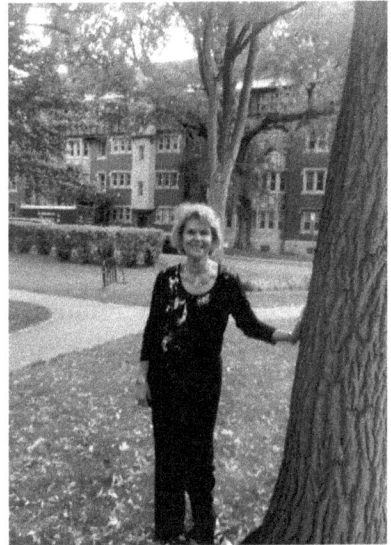

Me in 2013 in front of the same
apartment building, roughly
seventy-six years later.

My parents continued to spend a few weeks in Florida during the winter even after I was born. Obviously, I went too—with my governess, of course! I had a live-in nurse/governess until I was old enough to go to school. We would all take the train and it would be at least a two-day trip each way. One time while we were in Florida my parents took me to a marina. Supposedly, I remarked that I had never seen so many boats in my whole life (less than five years)—it was supposed to be very cute and the story was often repeated.

Here I am with my parents Sam and Evelyn in Florida. I'm more interested in what my father is holding than having my picture taken.

In 1937, when I was two and a half, we moved to a duplex at 4869 Grosvenor. Some things never change. Like Andre, I played with a scooter. Ours were a lot simpler than the "Razors" of today. I also had a stuffed dog that I took with me everywhere. We now had our own backyard where I could play with neighbourhood friends. When Toby stayed with us we shared a room. It was not typical for women to smoke, especially grandmothers. Toby did, and when I was seven, she taught me how to use her cigarette-rolling machine. Imagine that!

On the same trip with my governess who was wearing a cap and uniform.

With my mother in our backyard at the house on Grosvenor the first summer we moved in, 1937.

My family was very small. I was an only child; most of my mother's family lived in Toronto and my father's family was all in Europe. I did mention in the last chapter that my father stayed with distant cousins when he first came to Quebec and

40

A few years later, when I was five and a half, in our backyard with friends from the neighbourhood. I'm in the middle.

This is what the house looks like today. It is exactly the same except for the new awnings above the front doors. We lived in the lower unit on the left.

The same summer (and same bathing suit) on my razor with my stuffed dog.

Left: This last picture, also in our backyard, was during a visit from our Toronto family. Beginning with Evelyn and going clockwise: Sam, Leon and Tiana (Evelyn's older sister), their son Murray (my cousin) and me.

that these cousins also had relatives in Montréal, Jenny and Lewis Kleinberg. They were the seniors of the family and they became my "grandparents" and extended family. We all lived on the same street. Their children, Queenie (my mother's best friend), Beatie, Dolly, and Jack lived in Montréal. Their daughter Sophie lived in Toronto, and their son Otto in New York. Otto was a renowned psychologist, unusual for a Jewish man in those times. Queenie married Phil Meyerovich and they lived at 5031 Grosvenor, on the same block as us. When Phil was just starting his law practice my father's business was one of his first clients.

My closest friend from that time, who still remains a close friend to this day, was Sorel Meyerovitch, Queenie and Phil's daughter As I mentioned, Queenie and my mother were close friends. They used to spend many afternoons together, either with us at home, or downtown once Sorel and I were in school. My

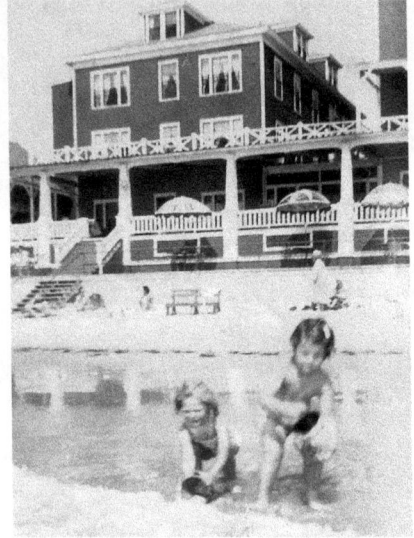

This is one of the few pictures I have of Sorel and myself as young children. It was taken in 1937 in Old Orchard Beach, Maine.

father would come home from the factory for lunch every day. After lunch, on his way back to work he'd often drop Evelyn and Queenie downtown and leave them to go window-shopping through the stores. In the afternoon, he would pick them up at the corner of what was then Burnside (now President Kennedy) and University, to bring them home in time to meet us when we got home from school. One day Sorel was unhappy with something that happened at her house. She was about seven or eight years old and she ran away. This could have been a serious event—a little girl wandering around by herself—but not this time; she left a note saying she ran away and would be at Esther's.

42

On Friday nights, the Kleinberg household was the gathering place for post-Shabbat dinner. Children of all ages along with their parents would gather. The women would bring cookies or cakes. Those were very happy Friday-night gatherings, and I have fond memories of that time. Even though I was not close to everyone in that extended family, there is a close bond between us that exists to this day.

In addition to Friday nights, we joined the Kleinberg's for Seder. If I close my eyes I can still picture the whole Seder table with everybody sitting around. Lewis, the senior Kleinberg, with his yarmulke and short white beard, was a very imposing man. As is the custom for the leader of the Seder, he sat at the head of the table with an embroidered pillow behind him. It made quite an impression on me.

My parents ran a very traditional Jewish home. We lit candles on Friday nights, went to synagogue on the high holidays, and kept kosher. I was enrolled in Sunday school at the Shaar, where I attended Hebrew class twice during the week and on Sunday mornings. There was a taxi that picked up me and about five friends at Iona Avenue School and took us to the synagogue. The first thing we did was go upstairs to the rabbi's secretary's office for chocolate milk before we started Hebrew class. After class, the taxi would take the same group back to their individual houses. I was friendly with Noonie Cohen Reisler, Farla Kellnor Grover, and Blema Solomon Steinberg. We all went from Iona school to Hebrew school together during the week by taxi and would take the streetcar together on Sundays. Classes were two hours. There was an hour of Hebrew and an hour of Jewish history. This gave us a very good education in Hebrew, our heritage, and the history of the Jewish people.

One Sunday, when I was eleven or twelve, Noonie, who was a real devil, decided we shouldn't go to Sunday school and should instead take the streetcar downtown. I don't know why we would have done this because everything was closed, even the restaurants. We must have just walked around and then taken the streetcar home. When I got home I realized that I didn't know if my father had tried to pick me up at school, which he often did. I did not want the lecture I knew would come if I was caught lying, so as soon as I walked in the door I said, "I didn't go to Sunday school, I went downtown." Whenever I did anything wrong (which was not often), I got a lecture from my father. I didn't get punished or spanked; I got a lecture. For any of you who've gotten lectures from your parents, you know it would be easier to sometimes get a punishment.

Hebrew school graduation in 1949, I'm in the first row, third girl from the left.

The night of Hebrew School graduation. Can you see the oriental print in the background? My parents bought two of these prints in New York to cover up some windows that looked out onto a brick wall. These are now hanging in our apartment in Montreal.

Getting on the bus for the Leaders Training Fellowship group. Leonard Cohen, the musician is standing next to me in the front row.

A highlight of my last year in Hebrew school (when I was fifteen) was being part of the Leaders Training Fellowship (LTF) group. We were invited to a conference in New York City! It was chaperoned, co-ed, and we travelled by bus. I felt so grown up going to the big city.

As I mentioned, we went to Florida for a few weeks in the winter until I started school. My school holiday over Christmas was too short to make the long trip, so instead we would go to Sainte Agathe (about sixty miles north of Montréal) and stay at Rabiners. When I was twelve we went to Lake Placid instead of Rabiners for our winter vacation. It took two trains with a transfer in Plattsburg to get there. By the time we arrived, my father, Sam, had come down with a cold, so the next day they called for a doctor. I was signed up for ski lessons, so off I went to find my class. I loved skiing! Sometime during my first day of lessons I fell and couldn't keep skiing, so I walked back to my hotel and even passed the doctor, who was leaving, on my way in. I got to our room, sat down, and explained what had happened. Believe it or not, I couldn't get up from my chair or even walk. Now we had to figure out how to get home. Two trains, all our luggage,

Our winter holiday at Rabiners in Saint Agathe in 1947. I had just turned eight.

My parents, Sam and Evelyn in Lake Placid the year I broke my leg.

and a girl who couldn't walk wasn't an option. We took a taxi home!

Once home I went to the hospital for an X-ray. Sure enough, my leg was broken. The doctor came to our house and put my cast on in the bathtub. It went from my ankle to hip, so I couldn't walk without crutches. Things got even more complicated. We used to walk home from school for lunch. I couldn't really do that, so I stayed and had my lunch in school. No one wanted me to be alone, so my best friend, Sorel, was allowed to stay with me. My father took me to school and picked me up every day.

Since my mother's family lived in Toronto, we visited them often. It was an easy trip, just one train ride. We would stay with my mother's sister, Tiana, her husband, Leon, and their son (my cousin), Murray. I would share a room with Murray, who was the first grandchild in the family. He was treated like a prince. I had to be quiet when I stayed with them, so I wouldn't wake him up. Funny how little memories like that stick with you.

When I was older, I would go to Toronto on my own or once or twice with Sorel. A porter would be paid to keep an eye on us on the train and deliver us to our family at the end of the trip. One year I was visiting over New Year's. I was too young to go out. I remember that Murray stayed in with me that night. It made such a big impression that he would do that for his little cousin.

Summer camp was a huge part of my childhood. I started going to Camp Hiawatha when I was five, in June 1940. I loved it! Some of my closest friends were made at summer camp, and they are still good friends today. (Think Mimi Kerman.) As an only child, it was wonderful being with a group of kids and having something to do all day long and through the evenings. I loved the athletics, the swimming, and just hanging around. My all-time favorite, once I was a little older, were the wilderness activities. The seven-day canoe trip was the highlight of the summer.

It was a very sheltered traditional Jewish camp. It was kosher-style. We had an Oneg Shabbat on Fridays and services Saturday morning. Hiawatha had a boys' and girls' camp. The boys were across the lake near the Weiner Ville Hotel (owned by the Weiner family, of course). Saturday-morning services alternated between the boys' and girls' camps. Our Saturday routine was pretty strict. We had breakfast, then went back to our bunks to clean and get changed into our whites. If services were at the boys' camp that week, we walked to it. Both the Friday-night Shabbat dinners and Saturday services gave me the knowledge and familiarity to follow services in synagogue and is probably why I still enjoy them to this day.

Camp Hiawatha 1941, visiting day. I'm between my father Sam, and my grandmother Theophelia. Hard to believe Sam was wearing a three-piece suit for camp visiting day.

The next summer in Weinerville, 1942. It's where my family rented a house for the summer that year. Left going clockwise: my grandmother Theophelia, my uncle Abe (my mother's brother), my father Sam and mother Evelyn in the center.

I was a well-behaved little girl. I was respectful, liked people, and was always nice. This was something my parents believed was very important. I followed all the rules. My girlfriend Farla was a little different, and the two of us sometimes pulled pranks at camp. One day in 1947 when I was twelve, we got caught and punished for one of our pranks. I don't even remember what the prank was, but I sure do remember the consequences. We were called down to the office, and the head counselor, Lillian Rabinovich Schrage, told us that our punishment was to live in the baby bunks with the eight- and nine-year-old's for a week. Not only that, we were not allowed to talk to anyone. I wish I could remember what we had done. Before the week was up I was called to the office again. This time Lillian said she understood that I had been talking. I really don't know what gave me the courage to say what I did, because it was not like me. I said to her, "I've always been told not to be rude, and when one of the kids talks to me and asks me a question, I think it's rude if I don't answer. So yes, I have been talking." Nothing happened—my punishment was not extended—but I still had to live in the baby bunk for the rest of the week.

Before the week was over there was another incident. I need to backtrack a bit to fully explain it. When I was twelve (in May of 1947), my father had a heart attack while on a business trip to New York. My mother immediately went there. I'm pretty sure she took the train, as air travel was not common yet. In those days, after a heart attack the doctors kept you on bed rest for six weeks, so my parents were basically stuck in New York for over a month. During that time, I was home with our housekeeper, Agnes. She was a very nice and capable woman. My uncle Arthur (my mother's brother) and his wife would often invite me to spend the weekend with them, and they sometimes took me to the movies with their children. In those days in Montréal you could not go to the movies on your own till you were sixteen. A few years earlier there had been a terrible fire in one of the theatres and over fifty children died in the blaze. So, it was quite exciting for me to be able to see a movie. Another thing I remember from this time was the long-distance phone calls. Long distance was not as accessible, and it was very expensive. I talked with my parents in New York once a week. Think about it. Today we use our cell phone to be in contact with anyone around the world through texting, FaceTime, messaging, WhatsApp, and Instagram. Imagine trying to explain the Internet to Sam and Evelyn.

In front of our house when I was twelve (1947) when my father was ill in New York City.

I don't remember being unhappy. I remember being concerned about when my parents would be coming home, but at twelve years old you are still fairly carefree. I had a very large circle of friends. We were still living on Grosvenor. I know he had his heart attack in May because I was supposed to go to camp at the end of June when school finished. My mother's friend Ann Rubin took me shopping for camp clothes that year. There are a couple of things that are interesting about this. First of all, it was the same Ann and her husband who adopted a child and inspired my parents to do so as well. The second thing was that Ann was used to spending more money on clothes than my mother spent. I vividly remember Ann taking me downtown shopping, where we bought a yellow one-piece bathing suit that was open at the midriff. I had an amazing camp wardrobe that year! I'm not sure who took me to camp that year, but I arrived.

Back to the second incident of my "punishment week." Queenie and Phil drove to camp to pick me up. The drive of about sixty miles took over two and a half hours with at least twenty miles on a washboard dirt road. When they arrived, I was still living in the baby bunk. They came to pick me up, so I could go to Montréal to see my father, who had just returned from New York. Lillian met them and told Phil that I couldn't leave because I hadn't finished my punishment. Well, this was all Phil needed to hear. He was a lawyer, a man of stature with broad shoulders and distinguished looks. He said, "Lillian, Esther has not seen her parents for six weeks. I am here to pick her up and I don't care where you put her when she comes back, but she is coming home to Montréal with me now."

I remember being a little afraid of seeing my father—what was he going to look like and how should I react? Needless to say, when you love someone, and they love you back and you finally see them, there are no obstacles or insecurities. I think I spent two or three days at home and then Phil and Queenie drove me back to camp. I went to my regular cabin and didn't have to spend any more time in the baby bunks. Years and years later, Lillian married someone in the Brownstein family, a nephew of my mother-in-law. When I had the opportunity, I asked her if she remembered the incident. Even though she didn't remember, it was etched in my mind.

Although my father's health was not ideal, his business was doing well and continued to grow. Sam was well known as an ethical and honest businessman. He rarely needed to sign a contract, as his handshake and word were his bond. His reputation was everything to him. He was also very loyal and generous to his employees. When World War Two broke out he continued to pay employees, who went into service and guaranteed their job when they returned. When there was a shortage of materials during the war, Sam often shared what he had with both friends and competitors, so they could all succeed. Julie Kates, one of Sam's salesmen, was stationed in England. Sam made the introduction, so Julie could have a home-cooked dinner with Sam's sister's family there.

Majestic employee Christmas Party in 1949. I'm on the right, fourth one in between my parents. My cousin Len is looking over my head. Rudy Corber is first on the left.

As I mentioned, my parents would go to Florida for a few weeks every winter, but after Sam's heart attack they went for three to four months in order to escape the harsh winters in Montréal. Mrs. Workman, a housekeeper/cook/babysitter, along with the live-in help, stayed and looked after me.

My father also felt he wanted to bring someone into the business who was family. He knew his sister in England had a child who was supposed to be clever, and my father thought he might be a good candidate. And so, he arranged for his nephew, Len Silverman, to come to Canada and join Majestic. He lived with us on Grosvenor Avenue.

I'm in front of our house on Grosvenor with Len.

In 1950, when I was fifteen, we moved from Grosvenor to Ridgewood Avenue, which was at the top of a hill. Our apartment overlooked the large Cote des Neiges cemetery. My parents had taken two apartments and converted them into one larger unit. Len moved with us too.

I went to Montréal High School for girls on University. It was a combined campus, with one building for girls and one for boys. We would mingle during recess and all-school activities, but our classes were separate.

I had a wonderful social life. I was part of a group of a dozen or so boys and girls. We used to get together for parties on the weekends. In those days, a party meant getting together at someone's house—dancing in the basement, listening to music. The girls all came on their own, as did the boys, but the boys always took the girls home. So, on Friday night you might have a "date" with Alan, but on Saturday it could have been with Herbie. We all hung out together and it was fantastic.

One day when I was fifteen, I was buying a pair of shoes at the Brown's Shoe Store on Queen Mary Road near Decarie Boulevard, and I noticed a new salesman who was really cute. I had my eye on him till I heard someone say, "Andre," and then ask him a question. He answered with an accent, and I just assumed he was French and not Jewish because Andre is a very common French-Canadian name. I said to myself, "Oh well, that's too bad," and continued with my shopping. Not long after this I was swimming at the Snowdon YM-YWHA (a Jewish community center) with friends, and who did I see at the pool? None other than Andre (who I thought was French-Canadian). Now I was really interested and had to keep going back to the store to get to know him. My poor father got so many bills from the store—a pair of slippers and a pair of galoshes were two items I distinctly remember buying during my "get to know Andre" phase. He finally asked me out, and for the life of me I can't remember what we did (and neither can he). But I absolutely remember telling my best friend Sorel that I'd just gone out with the man I was going to marry. I was fifteen years old and most likely if any of you came home and told your parents (I wouldn't tell mine, I told a friend) that you were going to marry the guy you just went on a first date with, you might find yourself not being allowed to go out with him again.

Andre gave me this picture when we started going steady. It was 1949, he was 18 and I was 15.

Look at what he wrote on the back: "With lots of love and affection"

I'll tell you about his family later, but for now just know his family had a country house in Ivry, pronounced Eevri, about twenty miles from Camp Hiawatha, where I was still spending my summers, though now as a counselor in training. Andre would sometimes drive over in Uncle Solly's car (his brother-in-law) to bring me to their house in Ivry on my day off. The car was never the same after driving the twenty miles to camp on the washboard dirt road. It was either Uncle Solly's car or Andre's brother Gerald's, but whichever car he borrowed it was never the same again.

Andre and Irwin in Ivry the summer of 1952 on my day off from camp Hiawatha. Solly's car which they used to pick me up is in the background.

Once camp was over and I was back home, we started planning my Sweet Sixteen party. Of course, I asked Andre to be the host at the party, which was held at the Berkley Hotel on Sherbrooke Street. It is no longer a hotel, but for those of you who know Montréal, it's just east of the Ritz and Holt Renfrew. We rented a large room and had a sit-down dinner with dancing. We didn't have live music. We used a phonograph that had an automatic machine where we could load twelve records. We must have been fifteen guys and fifteen gals, and it was a great party.

I'm cutting the cake at my sweet 16 party. Andre has his eye on his steady girlfriend.

Now I'm seventeen and its New Year's Eve. Andre's family had gone up to their country house in Ivry. We were going to have a few couples over to Andre's for a party. Andre and I were one couple, his brother Irwin and his date another. We went shopping for food and even though we were only going to have six or eight people, we bought food for twenty. I have no idea why we bought so much food. We did not plan on serving liquor, just soft drinks and the delicatessen food we had purchased. We started off the evening with just eight of us. Before we knew it, and by the time the whole evening was over, we must have had a hundred and fifty people come to the party. At about three o'clock in the morning, the phone rang. It was for me. When I picked up the phone I heard my father say, "Don't you think it's time to come home, young lady?" Needless to say, Andre brought me home rather quickly. The following morning one of my girlfriends called to see if it was OK for Andre to call the house. Andre did call, and as you can see the romance was not terminated.

We would go to movies with Irwin and his date or with Sorel, my best friend, and Ralph, who would become her husband. Every Sunday night we would go out for Chinese food with Irwin and we made sure I was home early to answer the phone when my parents called from Florida. In the winter, we would go skating at Blue Bonnets or skiing with friends.

This picture is a good example of how we hung out with friends. Andre is lying on the grass in front of the group and I am sitting beside him.

Here we are skating at Blue Bonnets

Left: This is a group of us skiing in Rawdon, Quebec about 85 kilometers north of Montreal. We are wearing leather lace up boots and have cable bindings on our skis. I'm not sure what the ski area was called back then, but in 1969 in became Ski Montcalm.

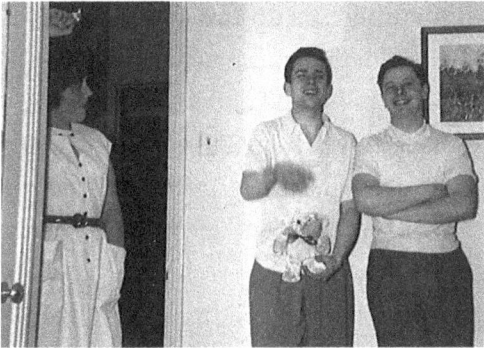

Andre holding "Andy Pandy" standing next to Irwin. My girlfriend Sorel is standing in the doorway.

One time, after we had been out with Sorel and Ralph and then gone back to our house, we lost track of time and Andre and Ralph missed the last streetcar and bus. They had to walk all the way from Cote de Neiges to Outremont, about five miles, in the snow. Another time we went to Belmont Park, where Andre won a stuffed panda bear and of course gave it to me.

I turned eighteen in October and Andre proposed to me in November. We were in the apartment on Ridgewood. He asked me if I would be the mother of his children. I thought it was a very romantic proposal, and of course I said yes. That was the easy part. Now he had to ask my father's permission.

"Andy Pandy" on my bed in his place of honor.

Andre was really nervous, but he came up with the strength to ask, and my father said yes. Sam was an excellent judge of character and even though Andre had a different background, he knew he would be the kind of person who would always look after me.

Even though I was engaged, I still had to live by the very strict rules of the house. In December of that year my girlfriend Farla was having a party to celebrate her engagement to David Grover. The party was to be held at his parents' country house in Sainte Agathe. I guess I knew my parents would not be thrilled about me going because it would mean staying overnight—and who knew "what might happen." I figured that I was eighteen and engaged so I could do what I wanted and not be such a goody-goody, so I never asked about going. My father sensed something was up and about ten days before the party he asked me, "What's coming up, any parties or events?" I tried to be as nonchalant as I could and said, "Nothing much. The Grovers are having a party to celebrate their engagement in Sainte Agathe." He looked me straight in the eye and said, "You're not thinking of going, are you?" I said, "Why not?" He said, "You're not going." PS, we never went.

I hope I have given you a sense of what my childhood was like. It must seem strange to you that I spent so many months away from my parents after my father's heart attack and that I was being looked after by a "nanny" during the winter months and then off to camp for eight weeks in the summer. But I never felt alone or abandoned. My children have often asked if I ever wanted to find my birth parents. I never did. I've always felt I had only one mother and father, Evelyn and Sam. This is mostly because I grew up in a happy home surrounded by friends and family who loved me. The other reason is the way my father told me about being adopted. When I was about six, I heard some of the adults talking about adoption. Before I had the chance to ask my parents what this was, my father took me to Eaton's Department Store, bought me a doll, and then took me for a drive. On the way home, he stopped and told me he wanted to tell me about the day I was adopted. "Mummy and I found out that we couldn't have children, but we still wanted a family, so we decided to adopt a baby. We went to an orphanage and were looking at all the children and babies. When we got to your crib you were smiling right at us." They decided that I was the perfect child. They could have adopted any of the children there, but they chose me because they thought I was special. Being told about it in this way really did make me feel special, because they had decided it was me they wanted, not just any child. I guess all my life I grew up feeling I was very special and very much loved and very much wanted.

Andre Landsman, five years old, Miskolc 1936.

Chapter Four:
Andre's Journey

I was born Endre Landsmann, June 1st, 1931, in Miskolc, Hungary, a small town about a hundred and twenty kilometers east of Budapest. My parents, Aladar Landsmann and Rozsi Ungerleider, and their extended families had lived in Hungary for several generations. We spoke Hungarian at home, though I have

Andre's birth certificate.

some recollection that my grandparents spoke a little Yiddish as well. You may have the assumption that most European Jews spoke Yiddish, but we didn't. Since our families had lived in Hungary for so many years we identified as Hungarians and spoke the language. I lived with both my parents and grandparents from my mother's side. My father's parents lived in the Tokay area and I was taken there only once to meet them when I was five or six years old. Ours was an observant home. Compared to Montréal standards today it would be considered orthodox. The house was kosher, and I went to services somewhat regularly with my grandparents, although if they had had their way we would have gone every single week. My parents, also observant, were so taken up with the daily needs of survival that they often could not make services. I lived there until I was five or six years old, when we moved to Budapest, so I could attend a proper school. Although I don't remember it, I was told I went to kindergarten in Miskolc.

Kindergarten class picture in Miskolc. No one looks very happy.

We lived in a small house on a back street in the main part of the city. At that time, there were no multi-unit or multi-story apartment buildings in Miskolc, though the city center was quite developed.

Andre in Miskolc when he was three. He is pointing at the person taking the photograph.

My father was a tailor and his shop was in the front of our house. We had running water (cold only) and electricity but no refrigeration. Remember, Hungary was in the midst of a depression when I was born, and the family was able to earn just enough to get by.

As I mentioned, in 1937 my parents decided to move. I stayed with my grandparents in Miskolc for about six months while my parents went ahead to arrange for housing and school in Budapest.

One of the very few pictures of Andre with his mother Rozsi taken in 1936 when he was five, before the family moved to Budapest.

We had a big family with lots of aunts and uncles and many, many cousins. It was very common for children to sometimes live with grandparents and sometimes live with parents or an aunt and uncle, as oftentimes people were in transition just trying to make ends meet. In Budapest, we lived in a flat at 82 Kiraly Street with not too many rooms.

There were a few loosely organized activities in the summer. It's hard to make out Andre, he is the one scratching his head.

The entrance to the apartment building that Andre lived in when he first moved to Budapest, and where he returned when he left the Ghetto is through the wooden doors. You can still easily see some of the damage and bullet holes from the war.

The inside courtyard as it looks today. Most apartment buildings were of a similar style with large open spaces in the middle. There were no interior hallways.

It was an apartment building with a large courtyard. It was cold in the winter and warm in the summer.

I went to a Jewish Day School. In those days, especially at the lower levels of education, the different religions did not mix in schools. Although it was a Jewish Day School, all of the instruction was in Hungarian. The religious aspect of education was expected to happen at home. In school, we did do translations of the Chumash and the siddur, to develop the tools to understand who we were and what we were about. After school, we would play with other kids, either in the schoolyard, in the synagogue's play yard, in the park around the corner, or out in the street. The area where we lived was predominantly Jewish, though by 1938 and '39 you were never mixing with kids of other religions regardless of where you lived.

There was a large market only a block away with both an indoor section and open-air stalls. We had no refrigeration, so we made a trip to the market almost every day. As the war progressed the

During the family trip to Israel and Hungary in 2009, we were able to access the building. Andre is speaking with a resident who cannot believe he ever lived there. He is laughing because he cannot convince her no matter how many details he has. When eventually he told the story of a jilted lover jumping off the roof into the courtyard and could identify exactly where he landed, she finally believed him.

quality of fruits and vegetables deteriorated dramatically. The market is still in use today and is also a popular tourist attraction.

The market as it looks today. It is a popular tourist attraction.

The same market in the 1930's.

Aside from the Jews, other groups in our neighbourhood were even poorer and couldn't afford anything better. Our family was at the lowest socioeconomic level. My father continued as a tailor in Budapest. Times were very, very hard and all garments were made

65

one by one. More often than not he would work with old clothes trying to breath a new life into them. Imagine, things were so scarce that before the winter, people would bring in an old coat. We would take it apart and put it back together inside-out to make a new coat. It might sound funny to you, but buttonholes were a problem because now they were on the wrong side of the coat. We would carefully sew the buttonholes closed and then make new ones on the other side. That's the kind of work we did to scratch out a living.

Even though the Nazi persecution of the Jews during World War Two had not yet begun in Hungary, there was plenty of persecution experienced in Budapest. Although the White Guard (government units who carried out a campaign of murder, torture, and humiliation) was officially suppressed in 1919, many of its most prominent members went underground and formed the core membership of a spreading nationalist and anti-Jewish movement, the Arrow Cross. By the 1930s they began to dominate the population in Budapest. Many of these young recruits dealt out their own brand of persecution.

A Jew being humiliated in Budapest. One Arrow Cross member questions him while another is pinching his ear from behind.

As I mentioned, we were at the very bottom of the socioeconomic ladder, along with our very poor non-Jewish neighbours. We were the scapegoats for all of their frustrations. Just for being a Jew you would get a kick for no reason at all. This was mostly done by teenagers. Adults wouldn›t bring themselves down to a child›s level, but they also never stopped the teenagers from dealing out their punishments. One of the worst atrocities to happen to children who had just started to read were all the proclamations that were posted on the street corners. You see, this all happened before TV was invented, and not everybody had a radio. Or, if you were Jewish, you were not allowed to have a radio.

Anti-Jewish policies and resentments grew more repressive in the years between World War One and World War Two as Hungary's leaders, who remained committed to regaining the lost territories of Greater Hungary, chose to align themselves with the fascist governments of Germany and Italy—the international actors most likely to stand behind Hungary's claims to territories lost after World War One.

In the beginning of the twentieth century the Jews of Hungary numbered roughly five percent of the population. This minority had managed to achieve great commercial success, and Jews were disproportionately represented in the professions, relative to their numbers. In Hungary, more than half of Hungarian industry was owned or operated by a few closely related Jewish banking families. In 1921 Budapest, eighty-eight percent of the members of the stock exchange and ninety-one percent of the currency brokers were Jews, many of them ennobled. Beyond the capital, more than half and perhaps as much as ninety percent of Hungarian industry was owned or operated by a few closely related Jewish banking families.

Jews represented one-fourth of all university students and close to half of the students at the Budapest Technology University. In the early twenties, sixty percent of Hungarian doctors, fifty-one percent of lawyers, thirty-nine percent of all privately employed engineers and chemists, thirty-four percent of editors and journalists, and twenty-nine percent of musicians identified themselves as Jews by religion.

Resentment of this Jewish trend of success was widespread: Admiral Horthy, leader of the National Conservative government, himself declared that he was "an anti-Semite," and remarked in a letter to one of his prime ministers, "I have considered it intolerable that here in Hungary everything, every factory, bank, large fortune, business, theater, press, commerce, etc. should be in Jewish hands, and that the Jew should be the image reflected of Hungary, especially abroad."

Unfortunately for Jews they had also become, by a quirk of history, the most visible minority remaining in Hungary; the other large "non-Hungarian" populations (including Slovaks, Slovenes, Croats, and Romanians, among others) had been abruptly excised from the Hungarian population by the territorial losses at Trianon. That left Hungary's Jews as the one ethnically separate group that could serve as a scapegoat for the nation's ills. The scapegoating began quickly. In 1920, Horthy's government passed a "Numerus Clausus," restricting the Jewish enrollment at universities to five percent or less, in order to reflect the Jewish population percentage.

Beginning in 1938, Hungary passed a series of anti-Jewish measures. The first, on May 29, 1938, restricted the number of Jews in every profession to twenty percent. The second anti-Jewish law a year later, further restricted professions to six percent. Employment in government at any level was forbidden and private companies were forbidden to employ more than twelve percent Jews. Two hundred and fifty thousand Hungarian Jews instantly lost their income. Most of them lost their right to vote as well. At the next election, less than a month after this new anti-Jewish legislation, only thirty-eight privileged Jews could vote. The Third anti-Jewish Law (August 8, 1941) prohibited intermarriage and penalized sexual intercourse between Jews and non-Jews. ("History of the Jews in Hungary," *Wikipedia*.)

These laws and other proclamations and edicts were posted on walls and street corners all over the city. They were all numbered and very official-looking, and they would tell you what you could and couldn't do. So here you are, a Jewish youngster. In those days, the culture was such that parents tried to protect and shelter their children. You had a general idea of what you could and couldn't do at home and what you could and couldn't do on the streets. As the war continued, and the Germans got closer and closer, these proclamations came out more frequently. Sometimes new ones every day. Now that you could read there was no protection from these edicts; you knew exactly what was happening. By 1941 the restrictions included wearing a yellow star. You had to wear it all the time, everywhere you went, so it was an invitation basically to get beaten up because you were identified as being Jewish.

Sometimes you would see a few Jews lined up outside a church door. They would go in, "get converted" and come out another door with a white star. Rather than this saving them, it made things worse, as you were now identified as being Jewish and pretending to be Christian.

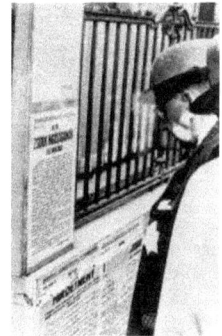

A Jewish man wearing a yellow star reads newly posted anti-semitic regulations in Budapest, Hungary 1944.

Reading was very important; it was basically our entertainment, and in those days what you were reading was literature or the newspapers. There were many newspapers that were basically cartoon and caricature propaganda against the Jews. As a child you would pick up one of these thinking that it would be funny and then you'd see it was about the Orthodox Jews being made fun of. You saw that so often that your mind got poisoned against them, yourself and your elders. It gave you a sense of insecurity about yourself and your surroundings. There were no discussions at home with your parents about this. It was a very confusing time. War was raging throughout Europe and as a child you almost glorified it. All you knew was based on rumors that you had heard. And that was based on World War One, which in some ways was like a gentleman's war. Though shortages prevailed, as Hungary was in a severe depression, food was available. Over fifty percent of the population worked in agriculture; the climate and soil were perfect for wheat production and Hungary's was some of the best in the world.

That is a snapshot of the environment we moved to in Budapest in 1937. The forced-labor service system was introduced in Hungary in 1939, the same year World War Two began. The system affected primarily the Jewish population, but many people belonging to other minorities were also inducted. At some point my father was gone. He may have been forced to join a labor camp; I just don't know. One day he was there, the next day after school, gone. A short time later, in 1941, my mother died. It was from an illness that could very possibly have been cured with antibiotics today. I have vague memories of attending the funeral. When Esther and I decided to visit Budapest for the first time in 1973, I wanted to visit my mother's grave. This took a bit of effort and perseverance to find. The gravesite was completely overgrown, as no family was living in Budapest to organize the upkeep. After that visit, I made arrangements with the cemetery for its maintenance.

Rozsi Landsmann, Andre's mother's, headstone. The convention in Hungary at the time was to list the husband first, Aladarne Landsmann, then sz to indicate the maiden name, Ungerleider, followed by her first name Rozsi. She was twenty-nine when she died.

On my second visit to Budapest, with most of the family in tow, it was very meaningful to me to visit my mother's gravesite together and recite Kaddish while gathered around the headstone holding hands. I know this had an impact on everyone there, as it was an opportunity to make history real.

70

You can really see how overgrown and unmaintained the cemetery is, though at the same time it is hauntingly beautiful.

The family leaving the gravesite after saying kaddish in 2009.

I was ten at the time and continued to live in Budapest with my grandparents Hermina and Armin and an aunt Ella and an uncle Peter, all on my mother's side. We lived that way for about two and a half years. I continued going to school and had my bar mitzvah sometime in my thirteenth year, late in 1943 or early 1944 at the Hunyadi synagogue across from the market. It was not a freestanding building. The synagogue was founded in 1896 and is located on the mezzanine floor of a tenement building today.

Grandmother Hermina, center in a Budapest park with Andre's Aunt Ella and Uncle Peter.

There was no party or celebration. It was a group of about half a dozen boys and we were called up to the bima together and each

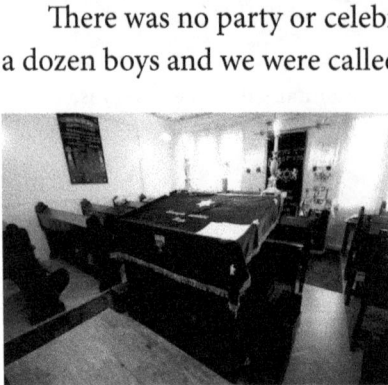

Inside the Hunyadi Synagogue. See how small it is, not much bigger than the other apartments in the building must be.

of us said a prayer. Even though times were very hard there was still time to play. Back then we also had scooters, but not quite as nice as the "Razors" of today. Ours were homemade out of a plank, two ball bearing wheels, and a steering stick in the front. They made a crazy racket. One day, somehow, I got a brand-new one from a factory. It had rubber wheels and was very quiet, no clanking as it went over the stones in the streets. That was no good. I wanted mine to be like all the others. It took me a while to figure it out, but soon I cut the rubber tires off the rims and now it was perfect and made a huge clatter going down the street.

Another episode I remember was the mailbox encounter. In those days, the mailboxes were mounted on the front of a building around four feet off the ground. I never noticed them because as I ran down the streets, either in Budapest or Miskolc, they were always over my head. The first couple of years we lived in the city I went back to Miskolc for the summers. One year, when I went back for the summer, I must have grown quite a bit, because I ran right into one and cut my forehead badly. Blood was streaming down my face and at the time I thought I would die.

On his trip to Hungary with Esther in 1973, Andre found a good example of the type of mailbox he ran into as a boy.

In March of 1944, things got much worse when Germany began their occupation of Hungary. The Arrow Cross was in charge by then and there were gangs attacking Jews all over the city. The German occupation in Budapest prior to the establishment of the ghetto was particularly brutal.

Hungarian and German soldiers drive arrested Jews into the Budapest municipal theatre - October 1944.

Captured Jewish women in Wesselényi Street, Budapest October 1944.

The first transports of Hungarian Jews to Auschwitz began in early May 1944 and continued even as Soviet troops approached. The Hungarian government was solely in charge of the Jews' transportation up to the northern border. The devotion to the cause of the "final solution" of the Hungarian gendarmes surprised even

Eichmann, the primary German commander in charge of carrying out the Holocaust. The Hungarians supervised their operation with only twenty officers and a staff of one hundred, which included drivers, cooks, etc. The Hungarian commander of the Kassa railroad station meticulously recorded the trains heading to Auschwitz with their place of departure and the number of people inside them. By the end of July roughly half a million Jews were deported to Auschwitz, where ninety percent of them were exterminated on arrival. Because the crematoria couldn't cope with the number of corpses, special pits were dug near them, where bodies were simply burned.

Arrow Cross Party members execute Jews along the banks of the Danube River, Budapest, Hungary, 1944.

During the same period, over fifteen thousand Jews were shot on the banks of the Danube River by the fascist Arrow Cross militiamen in Budapest. The Jews were tied together, ordered to take off their shoes, and shot at the edge of the water so that their bodies fell into the river like dominos and were carried away, saving the effort of disposing of the corpses.

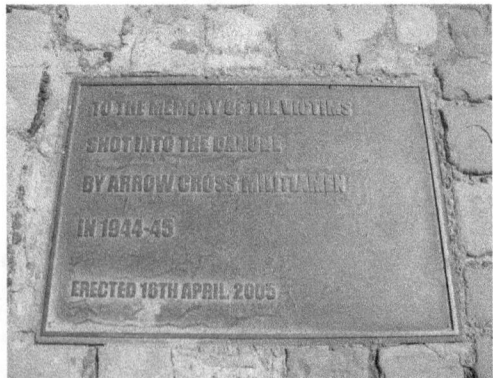

The Shoes on the Danube Bank is a memorial in Budapest, to honour the people who were killed by fascist Arrow Cross militiamen during World War II. It represents their shoes left behind on the bank.

We were also subject to random looting. A gang of hoodlums or the Arrow Cross could come into your building at any time and steal whatever they wanted. I remember one night sitting in the courtyard of our building when a gang with guns and sticks came in and demanded we fill their tin with any jewelry we had. They threatened we would be shot if they found anything we had hid. We handed over what we had and spent the rest of the night in the courtyard. When morning arrived, we could see they had left.

In November of 1944, not too long before the end of the war, the ghetto was established, and we were forced to move. The designated ghetto area was about twenty-five city blocks, not too far from where we had been living, with only a handful of openings to the outside world.

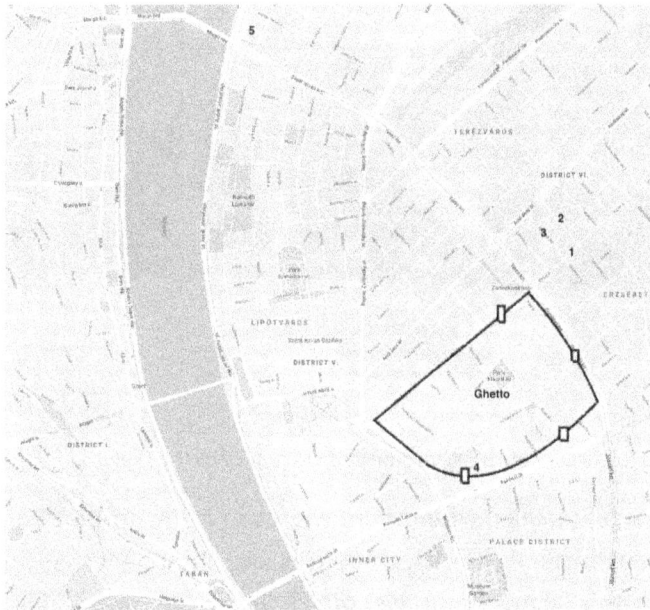

Budapest Ghetto 1944. The white rectangles are the four guarded entrances. 1 Andre's apartment at 82 Kiraly 2 Hunyadi synagogue where Andre had his Bar Mitzvah 3 Hunyadi market where the family did most of their shopping 4 The Dohány Street Synagogue, also known as the Great Synagogue or Tabakgasse Synagogue, is a historical building in Budapest, Hungary. It is the largest synagogue in Europe and the second largest in the world. 5 The International Ghetto.

The entrances of the ghetto were guarded by soldiers and young hoodlums to prevent smuggling food into the ghetto and Jews out. We were eight or more to a room, sleeping on mattresses on the floor. As I recall, hygiene was not a problem, though as a fourteen-year-old boy I probably didn't set the bar very high. Food was a day-to-day affair, more or less communal. Life was a meal-to-meal, day-to-day existence. Certain passes that allowed you to leave for a few hours or for the day were available, but you were restricted to living in the ghetto. In some ways, you wanted to stay in the ghetto because if you left you were likely to get beat up or worse.

One of the four guarded entrances to the Ghetto.

After a few weeks, when there was even more air bombardment over the outskirts of the city, there was one stinky job that I worked at. An abattoir (slaughterhouse) got shelled or bombed—I'm not sure—and somehow a work gang was organized and sanctioned by the Arrow Cross. They had the idea of rebuilding the abattoir, so our job was to work brick by brick, chiseling the cement off and then re-stacking the bricks so they could be reused. They took a bunch of us teens who wanted to work; it was totally voluntary. The place just stank with all the rotting carcasses in the destroyed building. At the end of the day we didn't get paid; we got a scrip. And with the scrip you could go into a store and get a bread and maybe some potatoes. You could also get some sausages but even in that time, with all the hardships, we would never even think of eating treif, non-kosher food. After the store, you hopped onto the back of the truck and went back to the ghetto with your bag of something edible. This job lasted a couple of weeks. I realize now that it was risky to volunteer for these work opportunities, as many times a group would be loaded in the back of a truck and never seen again.

There were other opportunities to leave the ghetto, but I rarely did. If you did go out you had to wear the yellow star, which left you vulnerable to questioning, beatings, or being shot. We were in the ghetto from November 1944 to February 1945, roughly four months, though it felt like years.

The shelling by the Russians in January of 1945 was a mixed experience. Here you were, sitting in the basement in the ghetto, hoping for defeat of the Hungarians and Germans, which also meant more destruction of buildings and Jews.

As the Russians approached the bombardment intensified, both aerial and artillery. We didn't know the difference; we were just trying to protect ourselves. You learned early on that if you heard the shells whistle and explode you were safe. It was the one you didn't hear that was going to get you. This lasted for a couple of weeks. We were hunkered down in the basements. Everyone heard when the sirens went off. I think if the Hungarians could have figured a way for no sirens to be heard in the ghetto, so the Jews could not take shelter they would have done it.

For the most part, the shells hit the roofline of buildings and destroyed only one or two floors. Sometimes a building would take a direct hit and completely collapse. In those instances, there was still a way to escape if you had been sheltering in the basement. There were chutes from the ground level outside on the sidewalks, similar to the ones in New York City, to the basements inside for coal and wood delivery for the furnaces in winter (though it had been several years since the last coal deliveries). We spent many days and nights hunkered down in these basements.

During the days, we would scavenge inside the ghetto. There was no school at this time, but I believe there were still services in the synagogue. I'll tell you this, which was amazing: somehow there was an organization of elected Hungarian Jews living in the ghetto who administered a small warehouse with some foodstuff, and from time to time if they had enough they would distribute it. I'm sure if you had means you could buy certain things, but I didn't know from that.

I'm sure most of you are familiar with Oskar Schindler, who saved thousands of mostly Polish Jewish refugees by employing them in his factories during the war. In Hungary, before the liberation, Raoul Wallenberg and others were actively saving Jews. As a Swedish diplomat, he led one of the most extensive and successful rescue efforts during the Nazi era.

I ran into some of those organizations. We were in between a rock and a hard place. We take information for granted today. We can question it, watch the news, and look at many sources. Back then you could forget about all of that. News in the ghetto was brought by native drums more than anything else. I might find myself in a place where I was told that if I went to a certain address it would be a safe house. The small "international ghetto" consisted of several "starred" houses under the protection of neutral powers in the thirteenth district, not far from the main ghetto. These were usually in better neighborhoods. As a fourteen-year-old you could easily sprint around and get to one of these houses in twenty minutes. Sure enough, when you got there you would see a poster with the Swedish, Danish, or Norwegian flag. The Germans didn't go into these places and neither did the Arrow Cross. I stayed in one of these for a week.

And then you would hear about a shooting down the street and that these houses were no longer safe. You didn't know if it was a rumor or true, so if there was nothing better you went back to the ghetto. These were not places where a child could get information. In those times adults didn't have time to talk to you or explain things. They were under too much pressure themselves.

It was a bitterly cold winter and then one day it was quiet. And that's something that's indelible in my mind as to how I found out that it was all over. It was February 13, 1945; there was an anti-aircraft battalion at the end of the street, right outside the ghetto. The firing from there was almost continuous. The guns were used so much that many exploded from overheating. When they stopped you noticed right away. As I mentioned, there were coal chutes for the apartment buildings. These were big round chutes built into the sidewalks with covers over them.

Half circle coal chute above the outdoor rectangular basement entrance.

As kids, we explored everywhere looking for anything. So, we were down in the basements and took a stick

Left: Red army troops marching into Budapest.

and very slowly started to lift a cover and peek out. We could see Russian tanks rolling down the street towards us. There was a lot of excitement and some cooler heads prevented us from running right out. There were still snipers out and the Russians were doing some kind of clean-up. Sure enough, the next day when we went out we were free and could also see the city was virtually destroyed.

Examples of the destruction and occupation in Budapest.

Lack of food and hunger was prevalent, both for the Jews liberated from the ghetto and the Russian soldiers liberating Budapest, as these soldiers had come from the front, where supplies had been limited for months. By then there was some retaliation by the Jews against their unsympathetic Hungarian neighbours. In those days, each apartment building had a concierge, and he was king. He had your life in his hands. He could report you to the Arrow Cross and you would be killed. In fact, the concierge was little more than a janitor, and when some of the adults got out of the ghetto they were quick to go back to their apartments to see if they could get even somehow. I remember that as I was walking out of the ghetto to our old apartment I saw a dead horse in the street and people were hacking off pieces of it. When I got to our building the concierge was overly friendly, being our best friend and offering a hot meal. It was soup with some kind of meat in it. I think they had gotten to the horse before us. I wouldn't even try it.

Another image I will never forget as the Russian troops came in were the women. There were women right alongside the men on the fronts. The women used their knives to cut off our yellow stars. To this day I regret not having kept mine and other souvenirs. Though at the time we were really looking to shed all these things. If I had kept mine, and I had a few different ones, I'd have had them framed. If I ever felt lousy, I could just look at them and things wouldn't seem so bad. The Russians did not have much to offer us, as they were coming from the front and were cold and hungry as well. Somehow things got organized and mobilized and there were bakeries where you could get some bread without having to pay. That's also when the looting started.

Russian snipers during liberation day. This photograph illustrates the garage style doors on the store fronts that they blew up and also the confusion of what might be inside the shop. There are no clues to tell you that Divatcsarnok translates to fashion hall.

The Russian soldiers began the looting by blowing up the locks on the garage-style doors with hand grenades. They couldn't read Hungarian, so they never knew what they were going to find. Once they were done, civilians could take what was left. On my way from the ghetto to our old apartment on liberation day I passed a store that sold iceboxes. I tested the weight of one, put it on my back, and took it home.

Another thing I remember about the looting is the toy store across the street from the main synagogue. The doors had been blown open and people were inside with newspaper torches, so they could see. The store caught on fire and completely burned down. You have no idea how much I would have liked to go inside.

An icebox, similar to the one Andre took from a shop.

When I got back to the apartment I found an aunt on my mother's side and a few other relatives. I lived with them. Schools and soup kitchens got organized. The Russians organized the communist party with some support from the Jews, who had few other allies helping them. There were also a number of outside organizations helping to restore basic services. I went back to school, a public high school, that happened to be all-Jewish.

About a year later, sometime early in 1946, someone said, "Look, it's not very good here and it's not going to get any better, you should come with us." I was fifteen at the time. They were going to America. This was a group of some young people and a very distant uncle. My decision was made instantly. Imagine, I came home from school and said, "These people are going and so am I." I took a few pictures and some other things I had. Any pictures you see here of me and my family were ones I took with me and have kept since then. I didn't have much; it all fit in a sack that was easy to carry.

We were a group of about thirty people. The adults knew each other. We got on a train. Whether it was a train or a streetcar, in

Andre witnessed the Hungarian Prime Minister Ferenc Szálasi given last rites before being hanged for war crimes and high treason, 1946. The execution took place in the courtyard of a large school. Andre and his friends were familiar with the building and climbed to the roof to watch the hanging. The method of hanging was unusual. A large post had a rope attached to a hook at the top. Szálasi was marched up steps, placed with his back to the post, his legs and arms were tied, the noose placed around his neck, the rope tightened, and the steps removed. For those not familiar with Szálasi, also known as the Hungarian Hitler, his hatred of the Jews was a pillar of his Weltanschauung (worldview). He seriously believed in the theory of a worldwide Jewish conspiracy. Firmly believing himself to be a good Christian and a Catholic, Szálasi argued that anti-Semitism was taught in the Bible itself. Unlike Hitler, Szálasi was merely an anti-Semite. He knew no inferior and superior races; he merely hated the Jews.

Andre's view of the hanging from the roof. An unknown photographer captured the hanging of Ferenc Szálasi, left. He and three of his former ministers were executed on March 12, 1946.

those times you just got on and didn't worry about a ticket. We took the train almost to the Austrian border. We got off at the stop right before the border, where soldiers were likely to board and stop us. Someone in our group had an introduction to a farmer whose land was right on the border. He saw us coming and led us to his barn. By this time, it was dusk. He told us to wait and that he would come and get us around three in the morning and walk us to where we needed to go. Sure enough, he came to get us, and we started our procession. We walked and walked and eventually he said he couldn't go with us any further and directed us to keep walking till we got to a train station. Half an hour later, dawn breaks and we are in a train station in Austria. There were other local people at the train station and I think groups like ours were a familiar sight.

We took the train to Vienna, where we were directed to a DP (displaced persons) reception center that was run by the United Nations. I had left everything behind and this was an adventure of sorts; at least I wasn't afraid for my life here. Just as an aside, while in Hungary the only second language you could learn was German. That wasn't something any of us wanted to do—learn the language of our oppressors. English and French were out of the question; if you were heard speaking those languages you would be branded a spy right away. So here we are in Austria, where the language is German, and we can't speak a word. Somehow with pointing and gestures we could make ourselves understood.

We had a couple of days in Vienna at the reception center and then we were assigned to a DP processing center with barracks outside of Linz. They arranged our food and transport on a freight train. From there I was sent to a DP camp in Salzburg. I was on my own at this time, as our group had been dispersed. I don't remember the details, but if somehow you got a few pennies and went into the town of Salzburg, you could go to a pastry shop and get the most delicious treats. Salzburg was a beautiful city that remained fairly intact during the war. On the other hand, we were angry as hell and had nothing, while it seemed as if the locals were fine and had everything. The reality was they were not that OK.

In the Salzburg camp, we were housed in Quonset huts and there was plenty of food and used clothing, though shoes were always a problem. Once things settled down the organizers realized that mixing orphaned children with adults was not the best situation, so they sent us to a children's DP camp in the town of Strobl, just outside of Salzburg. It was on an old estate and was in the most beautiful setting; it was breathtaking.

Aerial map of the Strobel children's camp.

When I got there in 1946 it had already been running for a few months. That's where I learned Yiddish, as it was the common language between most of the refugees. There were several people from different agencies that helped run the children's camp. There was a representative from Israel and a shaliah (someone usually sent from Israel to teach and interact with the local community with the purpose of instilling Jewish values and a strong feeling of commitment to Israel). He was a nice, nice young soldier. There was also a couple from England under the auspices of the American Jewish Joint Distribution Committee, also known as the JDC. They were lovely, decent people. There were a couple of survivors from Poland who were teachers by profession. They organized a school where the older kids were on staff and helped teach. Everything was done in Yiddish. There were seventy-five to one hundred children in the camp. I was the only Hungarian. Everyone came with different experiences. Some were barely literate, and we tried to bring them up to speed. I was the math teacher.

One of the few photographs of Andre in the camp, standing far right.

I was at this camp for about one year when I was fifteen to sixteen. Life was as decent as it could have been in an institution like this. When it was Passover, we had plenty of matzoh, though when Passover was finished it might take a few weeks till we got bread again. Many of the supplies were GI rations, so there were two-gallon tins of peanut butter. That may sound good but even a child can get tired of it. We were all friends and made the best of it. Communication wasn't always easy, but we managed. Imagine, we were a group of teenagers and finally there was some stability and safety; it was easy to make the best of it.

Let me go back a bit. I mentioned the shaliah. He was a loving, beautiful guy. I wish I remembered his name. He was very understanding. He tried to convince us that our future was in Israel. A lot of people were ready to go. He was honest about the process. From Austria, you had to go to Cyprus (and again be in some type of camp) and there was no guarantee of how long you would be there before you could go on to Israel. So, I said to him, "Look, I've been in the ghetto, and before that it was a smaller ghetto, and now I am here, always with a fence around me, and I can't take it anymore." He didn't argue with me. In the end, he did take a group to Israel by way of Cyprus.

Now, one day, another representative came to the camp. They said, "If you want to go to America it is going to take a long time. But if you want to go to Canada it will be shorter." I asked, "Where's Canada," and I looked at the map and said, "I'm going." There were eight or nine of us who were ready to go. We had our pictures taken and filled out some documents, then promptly forgot about it. Even though we forgot about it, there were many people working on our behalf to get the documents we would need to leave. Our sense of time was different; we didn't have calendars reminding us when to do things. Time passed based on the seasons and holidays, not individual days. Sure enough, in the winter of 1947, someone came back to the camp and said, "You're leaving tomorrow." We said goodbye to the others in the camp and again boarded a train, this time for Bremen. From there we boarded a boat for Halifax. I suppose that the effort to get us from the camp to the boat was done by the UN. Bringing us to Canada was done by the Jewish Immigrant Aid Society, more commonly known as JIAS.

We were each assigned a hammock (just like you see in the movies). Meals were served army-style with metal trays that had different shapes pressed in. You could eat as much as you wanted—till you would burst. It was the first time I saw dry cereal

The group of children from the camp who chose to go to Canada. Andre, second from the left, is wearing the fresh clothes they were all given.

Andre, second from left, in a farewell picture with many of the staff from the camp.

for breakfast; I never even knew that such a thing existed. It was a long journey that must have taken ten to twelve days. It was in the winter, so it was quite cold and often stormy. You can imagine that food was very important. I remember standing and eating something when I noticed a jar of pickles on the counter. They were small and very green. I thought, fantastic, so I reached in and got one. When I took a bite, it was the first time I got seasick and had to rush from the bottom of the ship all the way up to the decks. It was a gherkin, a sweet pickle. I was expecting a kosher sour dill pickle, something I hadn't seen since I was a really young child living in Miskolc. Since then I have never eaten a sweet pickle!

Andre, in the bitter cold, arriving Halifax 1947. He is leaving his sad and wandering story behind and beginning his new life.

Aside from the weather the voyage was uneventful. We arrived in Halifax. It was late December 1947 and that morning when we docked it was bitterly cold. It was the first time I had experienced cold like this. No matter how someone describes it, you can't appreciate it until you have experienced it yourself. We went from the boat into the station. We have our papers and there are people greeting us.

I should mention that in Bremen some other groups had joined us, so now we were about thirty in our children's group. We were all youngsters without parents. There was a leader assigned to us and we were told to wait for the train. We boarded in the afternoon and I have to say this was the most amazing trip. I'm not sure we understood the significance, but we had first-class tickets. The train, which was going across country and dropping us off in various cities, was overnight and we had the pull-down berths to sleep in. There were mattresses, sheets, and blankets—something unheard of during the war. Later in the afternoon, a uniformed porter came through and asked us which dinner seating we would like. When we got to the dining room each table was set with tablecloths, starched napkins, china, and cutlery. We thought we were in the lap of luxury. The last time any of us had seen this was before the war. It reminded me of the last Shabbat dinner I had had with my family years ago. It was truly an emotional moment. They even had a menu, which was unheard of. We had been happy just getting something to eat, never mind having a choice. The menu was in English and I was able to read most of it, but still I couldn't conceive of having these choices. Remember I mentioned the couple from England. They noticed how curious I was and gave me some self-teaching books for English— and that is how I learned English in the camp.

On the second day of the trip our leader, who had a list of all of us with the stops we were each supposed to get off at, started telling us where we were going. One to Moncton, another Quebec City, another Sherbrooke, another Montréal, and on and on. Finally, he gets to my name and says Regina. I say Regina, what's Regina—I don't know anything from this. I was one of the older kids and I said to the leader that I wasn't going to Regina, that I was going to Montréal. He said not possible, there are too many for Montréal as it is. I was very persistent, and he took out his pen, crossed out a few lines, and now I was going to Montréal and someone else to Regina.

There was a family of two brothers and a sister at the camp whom I was friendly with who were assigned to a stop out west. No matter how close we had been, once you got off the train that was all over. We were starting a new life. Of course, even if we had wanted to, there was no easy way to stay in touch with each other.

91

We were met at the station in Montréal and taken to the Herzl center on Jean Mance, just behind where the Y used to be. This was a holding and reception area for the children who had been sponsored by JIAS. We were met there by some representatives, some elders of the community, and there were even some newspaper reporters. We were probably the third group to arrive, so a little bit of old news. We were exceptionally well treated. It was understood that you were to be at the reception center for a short time, that the next group might come any day and there needed to be room for them. It was not done in a harsh manner; it was just understood. I was given a business card for J. Shreter's, a clothing store on St. Lawrence Street. When I got to the store, the owner, Joe, greeted me very warmly, as he was also of Hungarian origin. He wanted to hear everything and had a million questions, which I answered. He kept pulling clothes off the racks, saying take this and take that. I could barely walk out of the store, he gave me so much. He was a most generous man!

The routine was that people came to visit us. These were families who had the intention of taking in one of the youngsters. Sure enough, the very young ones, who were viewed as easier to integrate into a family, got placed. By this time, I was seventeen. So already I wasn't a baby anymore, and I was not taken. Instead, I was billeted with a couple who had a new apartment on Park Extension. They had just moved in and had a spare room, so I lived there for a few months. They were the Berlins, a lovely young couple with a one-year-old and another on the way. I think they had just moved from the States, as he had gotten a good job in Montréal. They probably also got a stipend for taking me in. They had a brother, Joe, who was in the furniture business and eventually became an executive director for the Shar Zion synagogue and then president of Solomon Schechter, the school my son Sam attended. He was a mover and shaker. I saw him again, probably thirty years later, under entirely different circumstances.

During this time, I met a gentleman by the name of Jerry Segal and he took a liking to me. He said, "I want to introduce you to a family, but they are not ready, I'll be in touch with you." Meanwhile, I attended Baron Bing high school. The staff and everyone was very nice to me. The students were probably ninety percent Jewish and the staff was not. They were very kind and tried to help bring me up to speed as much as they could. Initially I was put in ninth grade as I started school mid-year, after the Christmas break. That's what they thought I could cope with. With the exception of some French and literature I was bored. At the end of the year I got an invitation to the principal's office. I wasn't sure I wanted to go. He said, "Look, we can see you are bored. Here are some books to help you catch up over the summer and when you come back to school we will put you in eleventh grade," which was senior year.

Meanwhile, one of the other routines for the newly arrived orphans was Friday-night dinners, which went on for a few months. You were invited to a local family's home for Shabbat dinner. It was usually a group of six or seven that was invited. That was very memorable, as one night it was at the Bronfman's, a very wealthy and prominent Jewish family. And another night I remember was at Levi Becker's home. It was the first time I experienced a one-on-one with another teenager, his son Hillel. He was my first real acquaintance.

Eventually, I got a call from Jerry, whom I had met soon after my arrival. This must have been near the end of the school year in 1948. He said, "The family I want you to meet, the Brownstein's, would like to invite you to dinner." I went there for Shabbat dinner. Minnie and Ben and all their children were there with their spouses. We were twelve at the dinner table. Gerald, the oldest, with his wife, Shirley; Beatrice, the one daughter, with her husband, Sol; Harold and his wife, Natalie; Morty and his wife, Bernice; and the youngest son, Irwin, who was one year younger than me. They served a roast beef. I had never seen so much meat in one spot before. It looked raw to me, so I had an end piece that looked more well done, a tradition I stick to, to this day. Before the meal was even over, my mother, I can call her that now—Minnie Brownstein, known by everyone as Mama, asked me if I'd like to move in with them. So that's the end of the story. Except for my name, I was a part of the family. They were my parents and brothers and sisters. I never looked back.

We lived at 6001 Wilderton; Beatrice and Sol had their own home in the duplex above ours, and the other married siblings lived not too far away. It was just me and Irwin in the house. There were countless Friday-night dinners at Mama's. I babysat for my nieces and nephews Howard and Jeannie, Beatrice's children who lived upstairs. Mama and Papa would go to Florida for two to three months in the winter. Irwin and I would often go to dinner at Beatrice's. Morty taught me how to drive and I practiced on Solly's Buick and the store's Chevrolet coup.

Benjamin Brownstein, my new father, founded Brown's shoes in 1950. He immigrated to Montréal at the age of fifteen from Romania. I thought I had great aspirations for further education, but whether it was a real concern or not, I felt like a freeloader and that I had to give back somehow. It might not have been right on my part to make that assumption, but I still did. So, I went to work for Brown's Department Store full time after I graduated high school. Even when I was in high school I worked at the store. Both afternoons and evenings during the week and full time on the weekends. Ben had a store not too far from school on St Lawrence and whenever I could I would work there. I didn't realize it at the time, but it was a good learning experience. I learned how to approach the public, which was certainly not my strong suit at that time. Morty especially watched out for me at the store and gave wonderful advice. By 1940 I worked up to the level of store manager for the Snowdon location on Queen Mary.

Andre, right, Baron Bing high school graduation 1949.

ANDRE "Lady-Killer"
LANDSMAN

Prot.: Pegory Greek.
Fav. Occ.: YOU ARE VERRY
funny.
Fav. Oc.: Reading.
Pet Aver.: Radio commercials.
Amb.: To get ahead.
Prob. Dest.: Getting ahead.
Act.: Class Sports.

Andre "Lady-Killer" Landsman, who's ambition was to get ahead.
He certainly succeeded.

There is one incident that I still remember. There was a door to steep stairs in the back of the store. We would toss the empty shoe boxes down when a sale was complete. It could get quite disorganized when we were busy. Then we would straighten everything the next day and take all the garbage out. I noticed something suspicious and upon investigating realized one of the employees was stealing. I reported it to Ben and the person was fired.

Brown's was originally a department store with clothing for the whole family. Then they added shoes, which were very popular as now you could get the whole outfit in one place. As the shoes became more successful the clothing was phased out and the family opened new shoe shops in local neighborhoods.

It was while working as a salesman at the store on Queen Mary Road in Snowden that I met Esther. I'd better let her tell the rest of the story, as she would interrupt me anyway!

Once we became engaged, Sam, Esther's father, asked Ben if I could work with him at Majestic Neckwear. Ben said, "If you need him, it's OK." And so, I began my new career in the clothing-manufacturing business at Majestic.

Esther and Andre June 3, 1953.

Chapter Five:
Esther and Andre

1953 was a busy year. Our engagement was only six months long and there was so much to do. Several of my mother's friends made luncheons for me. They were much like bridal showers today.

Wedding dresses were still handmade, so I had a few trips to the dressmaker selecting the style and fabrics, and of course fittings. I was registered at Birks—a Canadian version of Tiffany's, which is still in business today.

Finally, the fateful day arrived, June 3rd, 1953. I was nervous, excited, and happy. We were married at the Shaar Hashomayim Synagogue. Can you believe the women were wearing mink stoles in June? Here's another anecdote: because the wedding was after May 24, it was acceptable to wear white. It was very important to my father that the men in the wedding party wear white formal jackets rather than traditional dark tuxedos. Andre did not have a strong opinion either way and was happy to agree.

MR. and MRS. ANDRE LANDSMAN, photographed after their recent wedding which took place in Shaar Hashomayim Synagogue. Formerly Miss Esther Harriet Cowan, the bride is the daughter of Mr. and Mrs. Samuel Cowan. The bridegroom is the foster son of Mr. and Mrs. Benjamin Brownstein.

Wedding announcement in the Montreal Star.

Ben, Sam and Andre leaving the Apartment on
Ridgewood for the wedding.

From the left, Evelyn, Sam, Andre, Esther and Minnie in
front of the synagogue before the wedding. Look at the
mink stoles the women are wearing in June.

Walking down the aisle was thrilling. I still remember Rabbi
Shuchat's words during the ceremony. The coronation of Queen
Elizabeth had been the day before and he spoke of today being our
day to be crowned. We were all more relaxed walking back down the
aisle after the service.

Walking down the aisle in the Shaar Hashomayim synagogue after the ceremony.

Left: My parents, Evelyn and Sam after the ceremony. They are so happy and proud.

The dinner was held in Kensington Hall, now Victor Hall, below the main sanctuary. This was before the major expansion of 1967, where the beautiful original entrance was integrated inside the new design. We had three hundred and fifty guests. What a wonderful family our marriage created. My mother's family and all the Brownstein's were there.

Andre's family at the reception. Top row from left Gerald (brother), Morty(brother), Bernice(sister-in-law), Irwin(brother), Beatrice (sister-in-law), Sol (brother-in-law) and Harold (brother). Bottom row Shirley(sister-in-law), Andre, Esther, Minnie(mother), Ben(father) and Natalie (sister-in-law).

There were two announcements in the paper. You'd think we were royalty with all the details about what everyone wore, including the suit I travelled in for our honeymoon. We didn't leave until the next day, so we booked a single room at the Mount Royal Hotel. It had a three-quarter-size bed and was not much bigger than a closet. It made no difference to us; we were happy to be together. The next morning, we flew to Miami Beach. It was our first time on an airplane.

Landsman-Cowan Nuptials

The second announcement in the newspaper.

We stayed at the Martinique Hotel and paid one hundred and fifty dollars for the week, which included two meals a day. We had such a good time, going to the monkey jungle, relaxing by the pool, and swimming in the ocean. At that time, Andre and I both weighed about the same. He was taller than me, very skinny, and looked quite young. I was a little heavier and more mature-looking. I was occasionally asked if I often travelled with my younger brother. It never bothered me; I was young and in love and just starting my life. Friends of ours from Montréal, Ruth and Morty Weiner, were

At the Martinique hotel on our honeymoon.

also honeymooning at the same hotel. At the end of our stay we drove to New York with them in their two-door car. We bought a roof rack to haul all our luggage. We stayed in New York at the Commodore Hotel for a few days, sightseeing and going to the theatre. From there we returned to Montréal on the train; it was overnight, and we had a roomette with an upper and lower birth.

The plan was to move in with my parents when we got back from our honeymoon. Andre was working at Majestic with Sam. We didn't have a car or much money. My parents still spent the summers in the country and winters in Florida, so we would have the place to ourselves half the year. Andre would drive to work with Sam or take the car himself when Sam was away. Living this way for a year would allow us to save enough money to move out on our own. I was also working at Majestic earning sixty dollars a week. Andre's salary was one hundred and twenty-five.

At dinner with friends at the Au Lutin Qui Bouffe restaurant in Montreal. A rough translation is "the elf who eats". The piglet was part of the restaurant experience. Although the piglet was saved from the fire, what appears as entertainment in this photo might be frowned upon today. The restaurant operated for seventy-five years before burning down in 1972.

In late October, four months after we were married, my father went to New York on a business trip with Rudy Corber, a senior manager at the company. Rudi was hired in 1947 and stayed with the company until he retired in 1989. My mother went to Toronto to visit her family. Andre and I were on our own and out for dinner the night they all left.

Unfortunately, my father had another heart attack and was admitted to the hospital. Knowing my father would need someone with him, Rudy decided to call me. They didn't want anyone to worry so they told me Sam had a bad cold and was recovering in the hospital. Rudy returned to Montréal and I went to New York, again on an overnight train, and rushed to the hospital when I arrived. I spent two days with my father. On the third day, November 2, I got a call at my hotel very early in the morning. My father had had another heart attack. Of course, I went directly to the hospital, where I was able to see him for a few hours before he passed away later that day.

Here I was, nineteen years old, alone and frightened with no idea of what to do. Of course, I called Andre and my mother and they both immediately flew to New York. I also called my mother's brother Abe, who lived in Paterson, New Jersey, not very far from New York. He cancelled all his appointments and drove to New York with his wife, Rae. They waited with me at the hospital until Andre and my mother arrived. We came back to Montréal on the train. It is Jewish tradition that a body not be left alone from the time a person passes away until they are buried. Being on the same train was the best we could do.

In those days children did not go to funerals or to the cemetery. My father's was the first funeral I had ever been to. Again, it was a frightening experience.

Right: Funeral notice and obituary for Sam Cowan in the local newspaper.

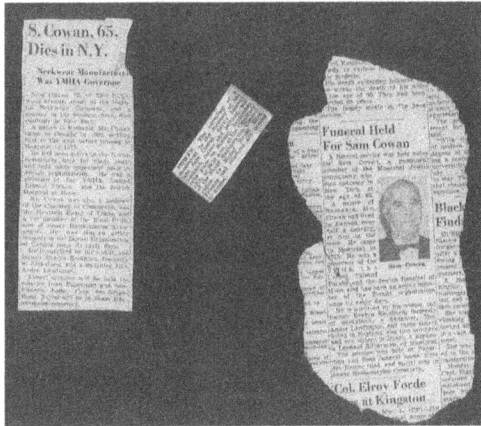

105

Andre's responsibilities now increased by three. He had me, my mother, and Majestic. He had only been working at Majestic with Sam, learning as much as he could, for less than a year. I can't imagine the stress, but somehow, we managed. My father had always looked after my mother. He did everything for her. She never drove (though she did learn), never had her own bank account, and never wrote a check or paid a bill. How strange it was for her to learn how to do this on her own. Andre was fabulous! He took care of her the same way Sam had.

We didn't have much money then and the rent on the Ridgewood apartment was high. Remember that we had taken two units and combined them into one. We found a duplex at 4695 Lacombe for one hundred and twenty-five dollars a month. It had two bedrooms, one bathroom, a small den, where Len would sleep, a living room, a dining room, and a kitchen. The best feature of the kitchen was the walk-in pantry with a window. In those days, everyone moved on May 1, but we were supposed get the duplex the beginning of April to help save a few dollars. To make a long story short, our plans did not work out and we had to find a temporary place to live for three weeks. Andre, my mother, and I moved into a rooming house where we all shared one room. We hung a curtain to give Evelyn some privacy. It didn't have a kitchen, just a hot plate and a small fridge.

After the rooming house, it was nice for all of us to move into the duplex! A year later, in October of 1954, I became pregnant with Roslyn. The summer I was due was

Although we didn't have much money for entertainment or travel we did make our own fun. We created an advertisement for Majestic products which had expanded their line to include men's smoking jackets. This is what we imagined a glamorous young couple doing at home in the evening.

the hottest on record. It was so hot that for a week before I gave birth I slept outside on the back balcony. Andre bought a Chrysler air conditioner, a real luxury, to put in the bedroom window. It was installed the day we brought Roslyn home from the hospital. In those days, you stayed in the hospital for seven days with a girl and eight days with a boy and then you had to stay at home for another full week after that. Wouldn't it be nice for women today to have such a long rest?

Back to the air conditioner, which weighed almost a hundred and fifty pounds. The electrician and Andre were barely able to lift it enough to put it in the window. As it was being installed, the clouds started rolling in, and by the time they turned it on it was raining. It cooled down and we didn't need air conditioning. Don't get me wrong, we used it plenty the rest of the summer. We also bought our first automatic washing machine. We used a clothesline outside in the summer to dry our clothes. That winter we had diapers hanging overnight in the kitchen. Disposable diapers hadn't been invented yet.

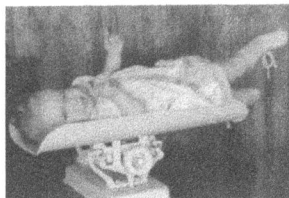

Baby Roslyn summer 1955.

Not only did we have a long rest at the hospital and then at home, we would also have a live-in nurse to help take care of the baby. Roslyn's nurse was Ms. Bedard. She would wear her official nursing uniform, including her cap. Back then, at least in Montréal, bottle-feeding was considered the way to go, so between feeding, bathing, and cloth diapers, there was plenty for the nurse to do. When Roslyn was born, Len moved out of the small den into his own place, which still barely left enough space for a crib and cot in the extra room. My mother, Evelyn, continued living with us, and did not move into her own apartment until we bought our house on King George.

In 1956, when Roslyn was one, we started our own tradition of renting a house in Ivry for the summer. It was a real, authentic farmhouse. I would stay for the whole summer with my mother and Roslyn. Ann and Lucy and Lou also came for a week or two while Andre commuted over the weekends. Our place was very close to Mama and Papa's, Shirley and Gerry, Natalie and Harold, and Joan and Jack. We were not too far from Morty and Bernice's place in Trout Lake, either.

We went in the winter too. Sledding in Ivry with Roslyn at eighteen months old.

Even though we were on our own now, the duplex on Lacombe was too small to accommodate a growing family, which we very much wanted. Andre's brother Morty was also looking to move and he found two semi-detached houses in a new development on King George, now known as Cavendish Boulevard. Wanting to know who his neighbours would be, Morty approached Andre and, voila, we moved to a brand-new house January of 1958 with Morty and Bernice and their three children living right next door. It snowed the first night we were in the house. It was a newly developed area with not much traffic. In the middle of the night the sidewalk snow-blower came tearing down the street at full speed and the house shook. Andre woke me up and in a nervous voice said, "MY G-D, our new house is falling down!" He was really startled. After that we got used to the noise. The house was considered very modern. It was a split-level with so much more room than we ever had. There were three bedrooms and two bathrooms on the upper level. The main area had a kitchen, dining room, and sunken living room. Downstairs there was a den/playroom, a laundry room, and an additional bedroom and bathroom for the housekeeper.

There was a lot to do to get the house set up and running, but we did make time to relax. Nine months later Tina was born! Times were good in the sixties and seventies. The US and Canadian economies were stabilizing after the war and businesses were doing well, especially at our company, Majestic. Friday-night dinners continued, and Passover was still an important event. Some of you may not realize it, but there are two Seders (first and second). One would be at our place for our family on my mother's side. Her sister Ann would come in from Toronto and her nephew Len would also join us. The other Seder would be the entire Brownstein family. Papa would lead the service and we never skipped anything; there would be a big search for

In front of our house on King George with Roslyn and baby Tina, spring 1959.

the afikomen, and then we would sing every verse of all the songs. It was a huge dinner, and as all the families grew, we were over fifty people one year.

After we were married, my mother continued to go to Florida for a few months in the winter. She would often drive down with Mama and Papa and stay in a hotel near them. We would visit all the grandparents and bring the children, though it was just for a week or two, not the whole winter.

Here's something else I remember: every Friday, before Shabbat began, Papa would go to the kosher bakery to get challah for all his children. There were six families to shop for. We would each get two big challahs and two bags of mini challah rolls. That's twenty-four bags of bread loaded into his trunk; it was packed. Papa would then drive to each of his children's homes to make the delivery. When Sam was old enough, he would sit on our outside front stairs waiting for Papa, so he could get a very fresh challah roll. Making the delivery wasn't so bad, as we lived next door to Morty for a few years, and Harold and Gerald also lived next door to each other in Westmount. One thing I haven't mentioned yet is that not only were Andre's brothers Harold and Gerald living next door to each other, but they were also married to sisters, Natalie and Shirley. That's how we got to know Joan and Jack Lupovitch, with whom we became very close friends, especially Andre and Jackie. Jackie was Natalie and Shirley's brother. It can get a bit complicated—Jackie was our sister-in-law's brother!

Another great thing about our new neighbourhood was that Joan and Jack lived across the street from us. They lived on Robinson, the next block over, and the back of their house faced ours with empty lots between us. There were so many friends and family within a stone's throw, there was always something going on.

It was after Tina was born that we caught the travel bug. In 1959, we went on an eighteen-day cruise to the Caribbean and South America with Joan and Jack. None of us had ever been on a cruise and we thought it was truly fantastic. The buffets were huge, the ports we stopped at were amazing to us, and there was always something to

do on the boat. We were in heaven. That same year Andre bought me my first car, a Chevrolet convertible. That was quite a night. We were out for dinner at Moishe's, our favorite steakhouse. When we were done and left the restaurant, Andre gave me some keys and said they were for my car. I was flabbergasted! He had arranged for the dealer to deliver it

Getting ready for formal night on our first cruise with Joan and Jack.

outside the restaurant as a surprise. It was one of the best cars we ever owned.

Next up was Susan, born in the summer of 1960. Life got really busy. Roslyn and Tina started sharing a bedroom while Susan and her nurse got the smaller one at the top of the stairs. We went on another cruise with Joan and Jack, this time to the Caribbean.

Susan and a neighbour sitting on the car a few years later.

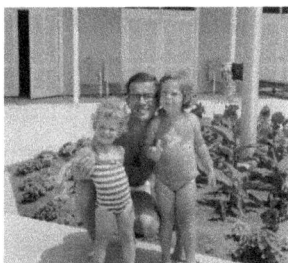

Tina and Susan at one year old in Deal, New Jersey visiting my uncle Abe.

Andre, Joan and Esther at costume night on our second cruise a year later. My crime was hiding the nightclothes from the steward and Joan's was wearing the same dress twice.

Andre was working to expand Majestic's product line. In the fifties, we added sleepwear. It was considered very chic for a man to wear a white terry robe at the end and beginning of his day and after a shower. Majestic sold terry robes made in their local facility to many prestigious accounts as well as the Canadian department stores. Bathrobes at that time were worn mostly in the winter. To keep sales consistent during the year, we added swimwear under the brand Surf King. We made bathing suits and cabana sets. Andre would travel to New York six or seven times a year looking at new styles and fabrics. Hard to believe, but all the garments were made in the factory on St Laurence. There were long cutting tables where the patterns were made, and the fabrics were stacked and cut. They would then go to the assembly area where the garments would be sewn together. Each sewing station had a special purpose: seams, buttonholes, trim, elastic, and labels, to name a few. The unfinished piece goods would go from station to station. Once assembled, the garment would be tossed into a large laundry bin and sent to the folding area where it would be packaged.

One of our expansions happened unexpectedly the same year we moved to a larger facility on St Viateur. Andre's sister Beatrice was married to Sol Krupp, one of the nicest men Andre and I have ever known. He too was in the garment business with his brother and brother-in-law. They made men's shirts under a license from the Manhattan Shirt Company. Sol was the salesman and travelled across Canada visiting all the menswear and department stores. He was very successful and had a wonderful relationship with his customers. In the early sixties, when he came home from one of his sales trips, his brothers declared there wasn't enough money to keep the business going so they were forced to close. This was a problem, because not only had Sol lost his livelihood, but he was not able to keep his delivery commitments to his customers. Sol's factory was shut down, along with all the unfinished garments that had no value to anyone until they were sewn together and ready for sale. Andre, Harold, Gerald, and Rudi Corber got together, formed a new business, and purchased the unfinished inventory. They had the facilities to put the garments together and honor Sol's delivery promises. Harold and Gerald, Andre's brothers, were also in the garment industry. They made women's sleepwear and their factory was in the same building as ours. The new company was called Luigi and came under the Majestic umbrella. Sol continued managing and leading Luigi until he passed away in 1978, a year after Papa.

A few years later, still wanting to expand, we purchased Caramy Knitting Mills and manufactured men's sweaters and pullovers. One of the lines was Leonardo Strassi by Caramy. We also had Jean Beliveau, the famous hockey player, as a spokesperson for the company. He modeled one of our sweaters and the packaging for it was thick clear plastic with a large insert of his photograph wearing the sweater. It was a sensation! It was a privilege to work with him. As we grew, we took over more space in the building. Sewing and knitting were on the second floor, with over two hundred seamstresses, shipping on the third floor, and cutting on the fifth. This was not very efficient, and we needed more space. We decided to build our own factory. Once we secured the land on Jean Rivard,

Sam (our son, whom we'll learn more about soon) joined the operation and headed up the new factory design and construction. In 1989, we moved to our new location. The facility was one hundred and twenty-five thousand square feet with eighty thousand of that dedicated to manufacturing. The warehouse, shipping, and receiving were much more automated, as well as many of the sewing functions. Although the space was larger, and business was growing, we only needed eighty to a hundred employees.

In the early nineties, Sam introduced our products to the US market, where they were well received. Although the business was doing well, things were changing. Manufacturing was moving overseas, and companies had to make adjustments to stay competitive. Though the space on Jean Rivard served us well for over twenty years, we sold the building in 2012 to Green Mountain Coffee. We then moved to a new facility on Kieran in St-Laurent with smaller production space but more room for our distribution needs to accommodate the new business model. Business travel changed too. Instead of trips to New York, Europe was a better market to see fashion trends, so we would go to different cities across Europe a few times a year. We also had to visit our factories and supervise production, so Sam started to travel to China, India, Bangladesh, and Cambodia.

Andre wasn't the only one working hard. From early on I was always involved in community service. It was a big part of our family life, beginning with my father. One of his mottos was "We do not live in this world rent-free; no matter how little you have, there are always others less fortunate who must be helped." Remember I mentioned the cigar case he received for his community service when he left Saskatoon. Seeing it displayed in our house was an inspiration to me to continue his tradition. I am proud to have it on display now for all to see; it is over one hundred years old.

I began my community-service career as a member of the Sharon chapter of Hadassah and became president the same year we moved to our first house on King George. There were several chapters within the organization. The Sharon chapter was involved with fundraising for Israel and other communities in Europe.

While a member of Hadassah I was asked to serve on the board of Baron de Hirsch, one of the agencies of Allied Jewish Community Services, AJCS. My participation in Baron de Hirsch was primarily in adoptions and orphanages. At that time, the organization looked after the social and financial needs of the Montréal Jewish community. Another agency of AJCS, Neighbourhood House, would have arranged Andre's housing when he arrived in Montréal. I could write another book detailing the history of the many Jewish organizations helping to support immigrants in Canada and the development of infrastructure and social services in Israel.

In the Sharon chapter, I began as secretary, then moved up to treasurer, vice president, and then president. I was also a national board member of Hadassah WIZO (Women's International Zionist Organization) and chaired the annual Montréal Youth Aliyah campaign and held several executive positions.

Youth Aliyah was founded in Germany in 1933 to relocate German Jewish children to Palestine pending resolution of the deteriorating political situation. However, as the Nazi resolve to eradicate the Jewish population became a systemic function, Youth Aliyah became a full-fledged child rescue effort. From 1933-1945, this "coalition" rescued 11,000 Jewish children relocating them to Palestine.

Since its inception in 1933, the mission of Youth Aliyah has not waned. To the contrary, since the end of the Second World War Youth Aliyah has continued serving Jewish youth communities globally including those in Ethiopia and North Africa, the Middle East, Eastern Europe, Russia and Asia. Today there are over 300,000 Youth Aliyah graduates from over 80 nations and Hadassah continues its essential support toward residential, educational, vocation and therapeutic services for displaced and "at-risk" Jewish youth. (From "Guide to the Youth Aliyah Records in the Hadassah Archives," *Finding Aid.*)

In 1979, after twenty years of community service, I was called into Manny Bashaw's office. He was the executive director of the AJCS, the umbrella organization of all the agencies providing education, welfare, health care, housing, and other services needed by the Jewish community both in Montréal and Israel. He said to me, "You've always been a bridesmaid, it's time to take the next step and be a bride." He asked me to chair the 1980 women's division of the CJA (Combined Jewish Appeal) campaign. He said, "Use your experience from the past twenty years and accept this responsibility." Andre and I discussed it and I accepted. The family was very supportive. This was the biggest job I had taken on and it was a fantastic learning experience and very gratifying. We raised two million dollars that year, the most ever for the women's division.

In the 1980s, Shirley, Gerald's wife and our sister-in-law, developed Alzheimer's. Harold, his brother, started a Montréal chapter within the Canadian Alzheimer's organization. Although we now had a local chapter it was difficult finding services in Montréal for Anglophones. Bernice, another sister-in-law, started a group within the Montréal chapter servicing the west end, which was predominantly Jewish and English-speaking. After a few years it became evident that this group needed to become independent.

Newspaper articles relating to my chairmanship of Combined Jewish Appeal women's division in 1980.

We became AGI (Alzheimer Groupe Incorporated). I held many positions in the organization, including president from 1995 to 1997, then remained on the Board of Directors and am active within the organization to this day.

Now, back to the family. Evelyn continued spending the winters in Florida, only now she rented an apartment for a year at a time, so she could leave her furniture in place. One winter our whole family went down over Passover and had Seder at the Hollywood Beach Hotel. It was a disaster; we all hated it, so no more Passover Seders out of town. As if we weren't busy enough, we joined the Elmridge Country Club in 1960 when I was pregnant with Susan. The next year, when Susan was a baby, Roslyn was old enough to go to nursery school, and then summer camp at Kinni Kinnik in Vermont. Her cousin Cheryl, Morty's daughter, who was living next door, went too. Camp was eight weeks long with a visiting day halfway through. We drove down with Evelyn, Tina, and Susan. Mama

Visiting day at camp Kinni Kinnic with Roslyn.

Me and Tina in Ivry sometime before Tina started going to camp. This was one of Andre's favorite photos.

and Papa also drove in their own car. It broke down and they never made it to visiting day that year. Imagine that, six years old and away for two months. That was common in our community; remember, I went to Camp Hiawatha as a child too. It was not long till Tina went to camp as well. Our travels continued, with another Caribbean cruise with Joan and Jack and then a European trip with the Gruenwald's after Majestic purchased Caramy from them. On that trip, we met my uncle Abe and his daughter Roslyn, who was attending school overseas. I know, it's confusing having a daughter and a niece with the same name.

116

We were starting to outgrow our house on King George. There were just enough bedrooms but limited space for the girls to run around. In 1963, we moved to Baronscourt, the first home we designed ourselves from scratch. This house was grand. On the top floor, there was a master plus four bedrooms. There was a curving spiral staircase

Construction at the house on Baronscourt 1963.

with a huge chandelier. We had a big kitchen, a den, a formal living room, and a large playroom in the basement. Again, there was a bedroom and bathroom for a housekeeper. This house was so modern, we upgraded from rotary dial telephones to push-button. The one outside the girls' bedrooms had a very long cord so they could stretch it out all the way to their room and close the door. That was handy when they started dating and wanted some privacy. We had a nice backyard that bordered Hampstead Park. The girls used to climb over our fence to get there. We were one of the first houses on the street. The Rosenbloom's had a home in the area as well. Theirs backed onto our street and we used to cut through their backyard instead of walking around the block. One thing to note is the house on King George stayed in the family. Sol and Beatrice bought it from us.

From the top clockwise, Evelyn, Roslyn, Tina, Susan and Connie Meyer, a friend of Roslyn's in front of the house. Construction was almost complete.

Life continued; we started spending more time in the winter with our friends Marilyn and Harvey Rosenbloom and Mimi and Merv Kerman as Joan and Jack went to Florida to escape the cold. I had known Harvey and Mimi for years beginning with my experiences at Camp Hiawatha. Both couples had three daughters roughly the same age as ours, so it was a built-in play group, especially when we went skiing.

117

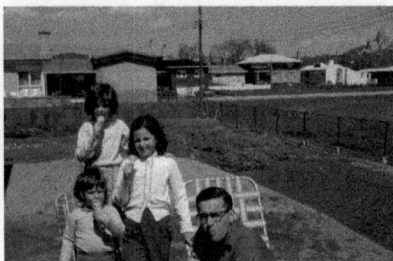

Roslyn, Connie, Andre and Tina
eating ice-cream (Andre's favorite)
before the landscaping was complete.
You can see the Rosenbloom's house
in the background.

Roslyn, Susan and Tina
having fun playing dress
up in the new house.

In January 1964, we went on our first European ski trip with Marilyn and Harvey to Kitzbuhel, Austria. It was magical! We were used to small T-bars and slow chairlifts at the local resorts outside of Montréal. Now we were in the big mountains with cable cars and amazing alpine skiing. The food was fantastic too, with little huts in the middle of nowhere serving homemade soups, bread, charcuterie, and wine in traditional leather wineskins. It was

In Kitzbuhel on our
first European ski trip
in 1964.

no surprise that Sam was born nine months later in November. Now we were done; we had a boy! I came

I wore the coat everywhere,
including when we
travelled.

home from the hospital to find a beautiful mink coat, a gift from Andre, draped over the bed.

I don't remember Tina or Susan's nurse, but I'll never forget Sam's. Her name was Carmen. She was French-Canadian, had red hair, and was really funny. She wore

118

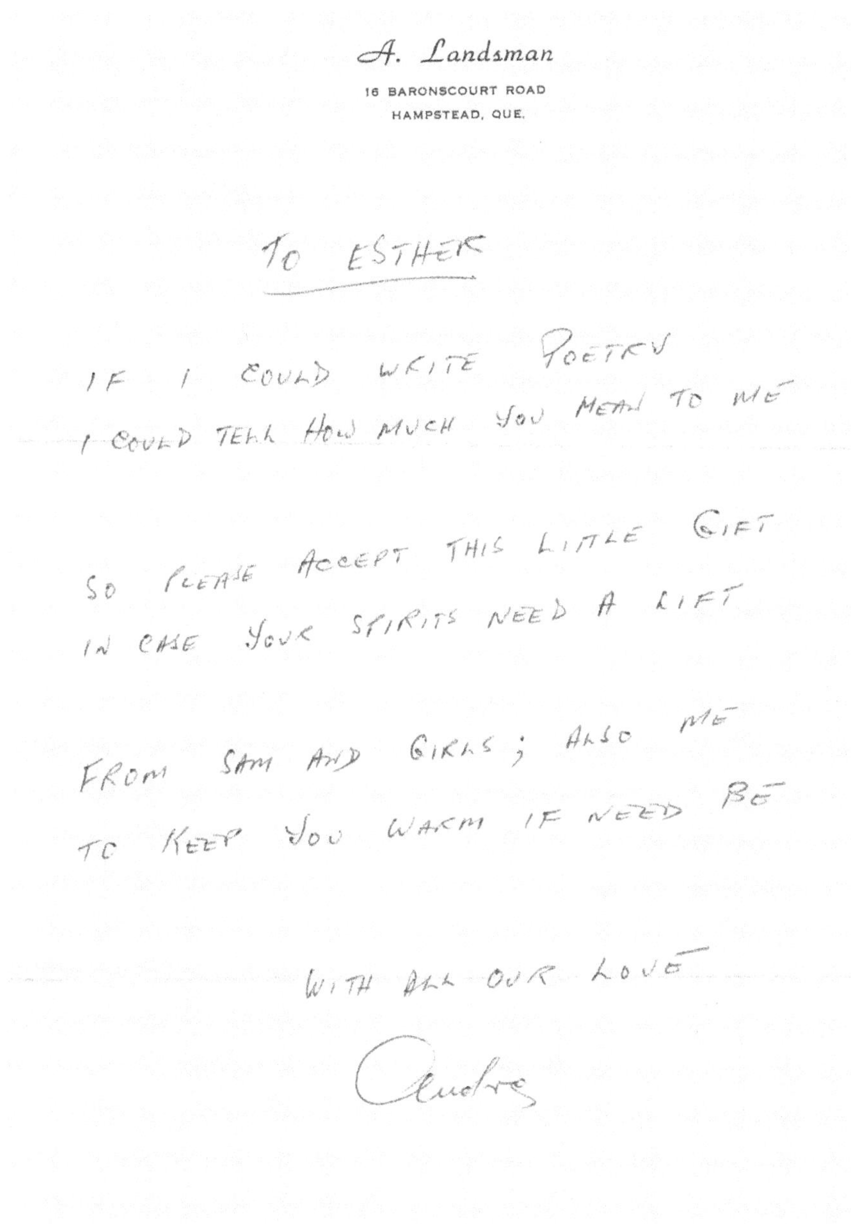

A. Landsman

16 BARONSCOURT ROAD
HAMPSTEAD, QUE.

TO ESTHER

IF I COULD WRITE POETRY
I COULD TELL HOW MUCH YOU MEAN TO ME

SO PLEASE ACCEPT THIS LITTLE GIFT
IN CASE YOUR SPIRITS NEED A LIFT

FROM SAM AND GIRLS; ALSO ME
TO KEEP YOU WARM IF NEED BE

WITH ALL OUR LOVE

Andre

The note Andre wrote when he gave me the fur coat.

these crazy false eyelashes with her nurse's uniform and recorded every single one of Sam's burps, farts, and poo. Andre reminded me that she weighed everything.

All the children had their portraits taken at roughly the same age. These portraits have always hung somewhere in our home. Clockwise: Roslyn, Tina, Sam and Susan. The resemblance between us is uncanny.

Susan, Tina and Roslyn with their baby brother Sam when he
was a few months old in 1966.

We also hired a live-in housekeeper, Encarnacion from Spain, whose nickname was Carny. She was with us for over thirty years. She became a real part of the family although sometimes we did drive each other crazy. Her room was right below the kitchen; if we needed anything at night we had to be super quiet so as not to disturb her. She did so much beyond cooking and cleaning. When Andre and I were away she ran the household, including making sure we got homework done, and went to any after-school appointments or activities. She was also very loyal and protective of the children. I remember if she needed to take Sam (her favorite)

Encarnation in the backyard sledding with
Sam and Susan the winter of 1965.

121

to the orthodontist they would call a taxi, so Sam wouldn't have to ride the bus. Though Carny loved the family, she didn't feel the same way for some of my friends. If they happened to be at the house she would make quite a racket in the kitchen.

On one of our many ski trips with Mimi and Merv Kerman.

We continued skiing in Europe every winter and Mimi and Merv started coming with us too. In 1965, Roslyn and Tina started ski school at Bernie Bloomers. Susan and Linda Rosenbloom went too. I would take them to the Town of Mount Royal shopping center on Saturday morning, where they'd get on a bus to Mont Alouette. Then I would go to my hairdresser, Frederick, in the same center and have my hair done. At the end of the day one of the parents would pick up the children. On some weekends when there was no ski school Andre and I would take Roslyn and Tina skiing. They started on the bunny slope with a rope tow. That was easy. Next was the T-bar. That was an adventure! If the kids were on their own they'd get lifted in the air because they were so light. If Andre rode up with them, he was able to keep everyone's skis on the ground, but he was so bent over that it killed his back. By this time Tina had her famous red hat; she could not leave the house without it. We sometimes went skiing with Morty and Bernice on Sundays. That was special because their routine was to order Chinese take-out when they got home. That was a treat for all.

Susan, Roslyn and Tina skiing. Tina is wearing her famous red hat.

1967 was a big year. Montréal was on the international stage that summer with Expo 67, a world's fair. We made several trips; it

The Kofflers visited us during Expo 67. We had a big bar-b-que in the backyard on Baronscourt. Sam is giving his cousin Tiana Koffler a kiss.

was so modern, as if science fiction had become real. We went to Toronto for Leon Koffler's bar mitzvah. Leon is Murray and Marvel's oldest son and it was a fabulous party. The girls had matching outfits, blue stretch pants with a red-and-blue striped top. Roslyn scraped her knee in the playground and was devastated that she had damaged her pants. We were able to fix them.

All three girls went to Camp Navarac that summer. To top it off we decided to get more serious about skiing. We rented a unit at the Farm Motel just outside of Stowe, Vermont, for the season. This was a huge ski area compared to Mont Alouette in Quebec. The Rosenbloom's and Kerman's rented there too. It was a two-and-a-half-hour drive with no traffic and clear roads. That rarely happened. Andre would come home from the office on Friday afternoon and change out of his suit. The car would be loaded with a large cooler

The three girls with Andre at Camp Navarac visiting day in 1967.

Like the girls, Sam also went to summer camp. Brant Lake visiting day
a few years later in 1974.

full of food for our lunches on the hill, our gear, and homework. We'd all pile into the station wagon and head out. I prepared a peanut-butter sandwich for Andre, so we could skip dinner and try to beat traffic on the Champlain Bridge. Then the debate would start on road conditions. There was no four-wheel drive then. The roads could be treacherous and sometimes it took over five hours to get to the motel. We'd ski Saturday and Sunday, then pack up and head back to Montréal. The girls all went to ski school. There was so much snow those two years at the Farm Motel. Our rooms were on the second floor and we could jump off the balcony into huge snow banks.

We ate dinner together as a family almost every night in the dining room. It began with salad served in the ever-famous half-crescent glass dishes, followed by the main course with vegetables and probably potatoes, then finished with a half a grapefruit, perfectly cut by Carny, and then desert. Friday night was the same, with the addition of my mother and Len. We said Kaddish and usually had roast beef. Tina even had a special roast-beef dress that she insisted on wearing Friday nights.

There was a beautiful crystal chandelier in the dining room. Once or twice a year Carny would take the entire thing apart and wash and dry every single piece of crystal. The girls always wanted to help, especially putting it back together. It was a huge production. Tina has one in her house and she does the same process too.

Another memory from that house is making wine. Even though we had made it on King George it was a bigger event at the new house. The whole family would be involved. Cases and cases of grapes would be delivered to the house and stored in the garage. Mama and Papa would always be there. Mama would supervise the operation. All the cousins would be running around. Some years we would pick the grapes off the vine but more often we'd toss the whole bunch into a grinder. The barrel would then sit in our furnace room to ferment and we'd stir the contents every few days. When it was deemed done, the barrel would be moved to cold storage. We used the wine on Friday nights and for holidays. We took it straight from the barrel into a carafe, never bottling it. Some years it was good, but we had one disaster and never made wine after that.

Len, my cousin who had lived with us before we got married and then on and off until Roslyn was born, was a bachelor and loved any opportunity to do things with the children. He would take them on outings, to skating lessons, to Beaver Lake to feed the ducks, and to La Ronde, the local amusement park. One thing they all remember is Chalet BBQ nights at his apartment!

Len with Sam at the amusement park 1967.

We enjoyed skiing as a family so much that we decided to build our own house in Stowe. We found some land and built a semi-detached house with Marilyn and Harvey. There was a door in the lower level connecting the two houses. The house was not quite ready for Christmas in 1968 so we rented a big A-frame house in town with Morty and Bernice and their three children. That was a crazy holiday. There were seven children, two boys and five girls. Michael, who was the oldest, shared a room with Sam, who was four at this time. Every night Michael would say, "What time should I set Sam for?" Sam was the alarm clock and once he was awake the whole house was up. That house was at the top of a steep driveway that was usually very icy. There were many mornings when it was a huge struggle with lots of pushing to get the cars out.

By the end of January, the house was ready, and we moved in. Though we had the same routine—leave Friday, come home Sunday night—the debate changed. The new house was at the top of a curving road. Even if it had just been plowed, we often didn't make it up the hill. There was many a discussion about whether we would

From left: Esther, Andre, Harvey and Marilyn in front of the house in Stowe.

make it and how much we had to carry if we didn't. No one, especially Andre, wanted to carry everything up the hill after a long week at the office and a stressful drive, even though there would be a nice scotch waiting for him as the house warmed up. We tried everything, including chains. Andre had a special (old) coat that he would wear to put them on, as it was a filthy job. The chains often worked but were by no means foolproof. We still had the same large green cooler filled with smoked turkey and cold cuts. By now, Sam was old enough to go to daycare at the beginner hill. It was not his favorite thing and the next year he was in ski school. About two years later, the Kerman's built their house in Stowe across the street from us. Now the compound was complete.

The weather could be brutal, and the chairlifts were slow. There used to be large blankets draped over railings where you got on the lift. The lift blankets were actually more like a poncho you slipped over your head. The outer layer was wind- and water-resistant and the lining was wool, usually hunter's red-and-black check. We used to measure how cold it was by how many blankets we needed to wear on the lift. The worst was a three-poncho day, two over your head in a conventional fashion and the third just wrapped around your head and shoulders. The goal was to form sort of a tent that wind couldn't get through. When you got it right you had your own personal warm space for the entire ride. Other times the ride was a long struggle to get the blankets adjusted to block the wind. Another thing that

On the Kerman's deck in Stowe, early 70's. Back row from left: Susan, Esther, Tina, Mimi, Andre, Merv and Merv's mother. Middle: Shelley Kerman, Janis Kerman playing guitar, JoJo and Roslyn. Front row: Karen Kerman and Sam

was different was that instead of a lift ticket for the day, we had little books with coupons. Each sheet from the book had six coupons, about the size of a raffle ticket. It was a big day if you had five runs.

The memories from those years in Stowe together are countless and I could write another book just about that. Sam and his family still use the house year-round.

At this point we had a routine and rhythm to our life. School from September to the end of June. Golfing as much as we could at Elmridge, skiing in Stowe every weekend all winter, and summer camp for the children in June and July. That should have been enough for us, but we got a dog, JoJo. She was a female standard black poodle, at the time the only hypoallergenic dog available. All in all, she was a good dog, though she often drove us crazy. She had us well trained. When we let her out she would run

At the house in Stowe. From left: Susan, Andre, Tina, JoJo and Sam.

128

around in the vacant fields next to us. She would have come right back when we called her in, but she knew if she waited long enough someone would get a piece of cheese to lure her back home.

JoJo also had an impact on our weekend routine. Sam used to sit in the front seat between me and Andre, often falling asleep with his head in one of our laps and his feet on the other for our drives to Stowe. That was now the dog's spot in the car, as she would be carsick if she sat in the back. No one wanted to deal with that so JoJo got the coveted place in the front.

Andre and I continued to travel. We had several European ski trips.

1975 Chamonix Esther and Andre.

One year, there was no snow in Stowe, so we met our cousins, the Kofflers, and their cousins the Zuchermans in Aspen. From left: Leslie Zucherman, Leon Koffler, Tina, Tiana Koffler, Sam, Marvelle Koffler, Roslyn, Adam Koffler, Theo Koffler, Murray Koffler, Leslie's sister is in front of Murray, Anna (Tom's wife) Esther, Tom Koffler, Andre and George Zucherman.

In 1969 Andre went on his first men's mission to Israel. The trip was organized by AJCS as a fundraiser. The itinerary included visits to kibbutzim, military, and historical sites with many well-known speakers. The goal of these missions was to expose and educate the

On the 1969 Men's mission. Moshe Dayan, Minister of Defense, spoke at one of the events. He is front row center. Harold, Andre's brother is third in from the left and Andre is right of center in the back row.

participants to the many needs and successes in Israel to bolster their fundraising efforts. In the coming years Andre and I went on several missions and in 1967 we went on a family trip with the three girls and my mother. Morty and his family were there too. It was such a success that in 1969 we went again, this time with Sam. It was during Passover and we had Seder at an army base. Sam stood up, belted out the Ma Nishtana (Four Questions), and had everyone at the base speechless. Being the performer, he also got on stage at a nightclub and sang again.

One of the belly dancers at the nightclub with Andre in Israel 1971.

Susan and Sam were both attending Hebrew day school and were able to speak Hebrew to the soldiers and their families. All were very impressed. We did have an awful experience one night in Tiberias. We were at a performance and Tina came down with a twenty-four-hour bug and got sick in the theatre. We left for the hotel right away only to find our reservations lost. Somehow, they found two rooms for the seven of us. It was a long night. The hotel didn't look very good at night and looked even worse in the daylight.

We were able to spend a few days with Yitzhak, Essie and Racheli Alexandroni, Andre's sister-in-laws cousins. He was a tank commander during the 6 Day war in 1967 and was able to take us to interesting places that we might otherwise not have access to. Clockwise from the left: Roslyn, Susan, Tina, Esther, Andre, Essie, Evelyn, Racheli and Sam.

Andre was a board member of the Solomon Schechter Academy in the early seventies. This is where Susan and Sam went to elementary school. Andre was instrumental in keeping the school running smoothly. At the end of the school term, the first year he was on the board, there wasn't enough money in the accounts to pay the teachers, and the school's bank would not advance the funds against payments coming in the next week. Andre called the bank manager, who handled Majestic, and convinced them to take on the school as a customer even though they did not meet the bank's fiscal requirements. He called a number of friends (mostly those who had children at the school) over to his house for a meeting and asked them to donate to the school. They also called many other families and asked that they bring over a check. Somehow, they collected enough to satisfy the bank and payroll was covered. Once the crisis was averted Andre and the board instituted many new policies that kept the school running smoothly. It might not seem like much, but credit was hard to come by, especially for new customers who didn't have enough in the way of assets.

Roslyn and Tina moved from the Hebrew day school to the local public school in Hampstead, where we were living. Susan was the only girl to continue in the Jewish day school system, attending Talmud Torah, Solomon Schechter, then Herzliah High School. It was a tough program. Not only did you have English and French, but there was also Hebrew. In 1972 Susan had her bat mitzvah at the Shar a Zion, the synagogue affiliated with Solomon Schechter. Several of Susan's friends who were just attending afternoon Hebrew school had a group bat mitzvah, but Susan was on her own and had a long torah portion!

1973 Susan's Bat Mitzvah. From left: Tina, Esther, Roslyn, Sam, Andre and Susan.

Sam was well known by all the staff at Solomon Schechter, including the principal, Rosa. Sometimes it was for getting into trouble and often it was for fixing equipment in the school. After a while Rosa admonished the teachers and told them not to call Sam out of class anymore no matter what. One very hot morning there was a program for the whole school in the basement auditorium, which was the only air-conditioned room. No one could get the projector to work. Many of the teachers tried; then they asked Rosa if they could get Sam. She refused, saying, "One of you must be able to fix it." Needless to say, they couldn't, so Rosa relented and asked Sam "for the last time." I think he was in fifth grade when this happened.

In October of 1977 it was Sam's bar mitzvah. I have to admit it was a struggle to get Sam to learn his portion, but he did a wonderful job. Unfortunately, Papa had just passed away, so we cancelled the big party for the adults and had something small at home for Sam and his friends. It was a bittersweet moment for us, sad over Papa's loss (though he had been sick and hospitalized for many years) and so proud of our son.

1977 Sam's Bar Mitzvah. From left Susan, Roslyn, Tina, Esther, Sam and Andre.

By this time, Roslyn had graduated from McGill and was attending the Wharton Business School in Philadelphia. Of course, she was home for the bar mitzvah weekend. That fall, Andre, Sam, and I drove her to school with a trailer full of old furniture she had repainted for her apartment. On the way, we stopped to see Abe and his wife Rae (Abe was my mother's brother) in New Jersey. Roslyn's apartment was on the second floor of an old row house. It was hot, and the stairs were steep. Andre saw two men in a piano moving truck and bet them fifty dollars they couldn't unload the trailer in an hour. That was the

Roslyn McGill graduation 1977.

cheapest moving expense we ever had; they unloaded everything, and Andre was happy to lose the bet.

Tina Mcgill graduation 1980.

In 1979 Roslyn graduated from the Wharton Business School and moved to Minneapolis. Tina graduated from McGill the following year and worked for Miracle Mart as an assistant buyer. She quickly moved up to buyer for the yarn and sewing notions department. I believe she still uses the knitting needles she acquired while there.

In 1982, Susan graduated from McGill and headed off to Columbia Business School for her MBA. She graduated in 1984 and first went to work in New York City for Wood Gundy, a preeminent Canadian investment banking firm. She soon discovered that her learning curve would be much steeper if she worked in a larger, more global firm, and a year later she moved to Solomon Brothers. She

Susan McGill graduation 1982.

worked there until a few days before she gave birth to Sam (Kimmell) in December of 1993.

Sam McGill graduation 1987.

Back to Sam (Landsman) who also went to McGill. After he graduated in 1987 he took some time off and went to Europe for the ski season. He landed up in Val-d'Isère, where he worked for the winter, and then went to London with some friends and worked for a few months. Joanne joined him in July; they bought a VW van and toured through Europe and Morocco. Sam went back to Val-d'Isère for another season, but that was cut short, as an opportunity arose at Majestic to relocate their operation. Andre asked Sam to come back and spearhead the project, which he did.

Groundbreaking for the new Majestic facility on Jean Rivard in 1989. From left: Seth, Philip, Tina, Sam, Andre and Esther.

The book may end here, but our family's story will continue to grow. It's been a remarkable and unique journey for Andre and me, who came together and created the family we are today. I hope you've found the story interesting, learned some new things, and are excited to pass it on to your own children.

For current generations and the future generations whom we haven't yet met, we'd like to pass along our own words of wisdom and core values. Family is a top priority. Keep your loved ones close and get along. Create events for all to attend. For the married couples, never go to bed angry. Value yourself, have the confidence to achieve your goals, and be the best version of yourself as possible.

We are so proud and love you all!

- Esther

So much to keep track of...

1981 Roslyn marries Bill Henderson. Family ski trip to St. Moritz to celebrate Andre's 50th birthday.

1982 JoJo passes

1983 Tina marries Philip Abbey

1984 My mother, Evelyn, passes away at 82

1985 Seth Abbey born

1986 Alex Henderson born. Esther and Andre move to Sunnyside in Westmount.

1989 Erica Abbey and Avery Henderson are born. Andre's mother, Minnie, passes away at 90

1991 Family ski trip to Whistler to celebrate Andre's 60th birthday

1992 Sam marries Joanne Borden. Daniel Abbey born. Esther and Andre purchase a condo at 2600 in West Palm Beach, Florida.

1993 Sam Kimmell born

1994 Michael Landsman born

1996 Ellie Kimmell and Alex Landsman born

1998 Seth Abbey bar mitzvah; Carny returns from Spain to attend

2000 Jonathan Landsman born

2001 Erica Abbey bat mitzvah

2005 Daniel Abbey bar mitzvah

2007 Sam Kimmell bar mitzvah

2009 Ellie Kimmell and Alex Landsman bat/bar mitzvah

2013 Seth Abbey marries Avigyle Grunbaum

2015 Erica Abbey marries David Rothstein. Anaelle Abbey born to Seth and Avigyle.

2017 Oren Abbey born to Seth and Avigayle

2018 Andre passes away May 1 at 86

www.ingramcontent.com/pod-product-compliance
Lightning Source LLC
Chambersburg PA
CBHW021828090426
42811CB00032B/2071/J